Football
Revolution

Football
Revolution

The Rise of the Spread Offense and
How It Transformed College Football

BART WRIGHT

UNIVERSITY OF NEBRASKA PRESS   LINCOLN & LONDON

Library of Congress Cataloging-in-Publication Data
Wright, Bart.
Football revolution: the rise of the spread offense and
how it transformed college football / Bart Wright.
pages cm.
ISBN 978-0-8032-7191-3 (pbk.: alk. paper)
1. Football—Offense. 2. College sports. I. Title.
GV951.8.W75 2013
796.332'63—dc23   2013019310

Set in Sabon by Laura Wellington.

Contents

Preface   vii

Acknowledgments   xi

1. Home of the Chokers (Late 1940s)   1

2. Team Starts with *T* (Late 1940s, Early 1950s)   17

3. High School Football (Early 1950s)   25

4. Big-Time College Football (Mid to Late 1950s)   35

5. Bear Bryant and the Coming of the Wishbone
   (Late 1960s)   49

6. Basketball on Grass (1970s)   61

7. Picking on Mike Singletary (Mid to Late 1970s)   75

8. Breaking Out (Early 1980s)   94

9. Turning Point (Late 1980s)   109

10. Settling In and Getting Out (Late 1980s, Early 1990s)   122

11. Changes, Even in the South (1990s)   139

12. Here It Comes, Hidden in Plain Sight (Mid-1990s)   159

13. Here, There, Everywhere (Late 1990s, Early 2000s)   179

14. Spirit of a New Millennium (2000s)   199

15. Full Circle (2012)   219

   Notes   235

Preface

You're going to find stories of origins of the spread coming from all different directions, because now it's become a marketing word. They market "The Spread" to fans, to the media and to the prospects. The size, speed and strength of defensive players has increased dramatically, so the width of the field has become much more important to us on offense; that's the heart of the spread. If you look long enough, like most things in this country, you'll probably find it started on the West Coast.

—DAVID CUTCLIFFE, Duke University football coach, 2009

Somebody once said the problem we have in understanding history is that our perception is unbalanced by our prior knowledge of the outcome. In twenty-first century college football, no single aspect of the game has more thoroughly undone everything once believed to be true than the development of the spread offense. More a way of thinking than a specific package of plays, the spread changed the way attaining success in the game is perceived.

It started in 1970, when college football's sphere of influence was much smaller and more limited conceptually. It was widely believed that all variations of moving the ball down the field had been explored and the best ones had been settled on. There was little difference from coast to coast, but in the West teams generally threw the ball more often, in the Midwest they ran it more, and in the South they wanted to do a little of each—beat you up with the run and then bury you with the pass.

The game has changed so much it's barely comparable to college football of the 1960s, 1970s, and for most of the nation's teams, on into the 1980s. The players recruited today to play linebacker are mostly lighter, taller, and more agile than those in the same positions thirty years ago. Safeties are bigger and more proficient pass defenders and they have a nasty streak; there's a new position on defense that is part outside linebacker, part safety, and part pass rusher. Defense is the part of the game that had to adjust to the spread—it forced defenses into a drastic remodel. For the offense, the spread brought all kinds of new players to the game—former basketball players, track athletes—generally speaking, it lured the best players to the game like a spider to a fly.

My interest in retracing this story wasn't in understanding why coaches started using the spread. That was obvious: it opened the field and made defenses play one on one. My curiosity was about why it took so long for college coaches who had seen the offense in action for five, six, eight years to make the switch. College coaches had been recruiting offensive players from suburban Los Angeles high schools for years, but those coaches weren't willing to try spreading out.

Eventually the spread was adopted by college football, becoming the base offense for teams at San Jose State, Stanford, and Washington State. Then later Kansas State, Kentucky, West Virginia, and others began surprising favored teams using the spread, sometimes in major upsets, and then it worked its way into the power center of college football. Championships were won, two spread teams—Miami and Washington—split a national title, and the spread was everywhere from the peewee leagues to the National Football League. These days every NFL team has some packages of spread plays.

Who were these first few experimenters? What mental makeup differentiated them from the hundreds or thousands of other coaches who had seen this high school offense on film and looked the other way? It turns out they were stitched together by a common bond of reasoning—common to them, that is.

They were outliers, about as radical as football coaches get to be, and they gave birth to an offense that changed the game and inspired others to take it and run—or pass, if they preferred—with it.

This is how it all happened.

Acknowledgments

This book took much longer than it ever should have and without the help of many people over the years, it probably would still be unfinished.

Mouse Davis, then the football coach at Portland State, first got me interested in writing more extensively about his offense, the run-and-shoot, when I was the sports columnist at the *Oregonian* back in 1979. He told captivating stories, filled with explosive statistical accomplishments, that were hard to believe until the following year when I watched his quarterback, Neil Lomax, throw seven touchdown passes in the first quarter of a 105–0 win over Delaware State.

Later I started researching what Mouse had done, when I was at the *Tacoma News Tribune* and my editor, Ted Pearson, assigned me to do a story on Dennis Erickson, the new coach at the time at the University of Idaho. Pearson, who grew up in Everett, Washington, was friends with Pinky Erickson, Dennis's father, and had been hearing a lot about a new offense that was going to make a mark in college football.

I couldn't have been more skeptical because the stories I was hearing from Pearson sounded like the ones I used to hear from Mouse Davis, and his offense wasn't exactly spreading like a wildfire.

Erickson, though, had a different presentation. He had played quarterback, had been considered a rising offensive coordinator among the veer offense supporters, but now he was an exponent of this empty backfield, spread offense that seemed to have an answer for everything.

When he won big at Washington State and then won more national championships and had a better winning percentage than any of the other coaches at Miami, I started thinking about some kind of book.

I owe my wife, Debbie, a trailer truckload of gratitude for her willingness to let me go work on this for extended periods of time. The book itself changed focus completely three different times, and each time I felt it necessary to take a week off from work to get it completed. I would pronounce I was starting over again, she was unfailingly supportive, and she needs to know how much that meant.

My son Brad offered constant support and encouragement to me, even when I was reporting another new start-up. He always told me I could do it, and eventually he got to tell me, "I knew you could."

The Erickson family, Pinky before his passing, his mother, Mary, and his sisters, Christy, Julie, and Nancy, all went out of their way to help dig into the depths of their past.

Robert Taylor, my editor at the University of Nebraska Press, was exceedingly patient as I stumbled through an unfamiliar editing format and was easy to work with throughout the editing process.

I deeply appreciated the time and effort Jack Neumeier granted me on several occasions to talk about the offense he created and the specific identification of the night he came up with the idea while watching a high school basketball game.

Bob Davie was immensely helpful time and again as an observer who saw the offense come into the game, and he had illustrative examples of how it changed things.

Kevin Steele provided the insight of a coach involved in the game when Washington State sent shock waves around the college football nation with a 52–24 victory that was felt by coaches from coast to coast.

Thanks to Patrick Smyth, head of the Denver Broncos' public relations staff, for helping arrange interviews with John Elway that led me to the funny story that until he played against the spread at Stanford when his father took it to San Jose State, it hadn't occurred to Elway that it was anything other than his old high school offense.

San Jose State publicist Lawrence Fan was a great help in assisting me with background information, including complete play-by-play packets from games. Others in college sports information who made this possible included Jeff Bechtold (Washington), Rod Commons (Washington State), Bill Stevens (Washington State), Dave Guffey (Montana), Steve McClain (Florida), Art Chase (Duke), Bill Lamberty (Montana State), Rick Korch (Miami), Tim Bourret (Clemson), and Mark Brand (Arizona State).

More coaches than I can recall were of great assistance to me, giving me time for the subject matter, sometimes in the middle of a season when the last thing they wanted was to get introspective and reflective, often at length, with someone they didn't know. But they helped, lots of them, including Gregg Smith (many times, many schools), Rob Spence (Rutgers), Dan Cozzetto (Washington), Homer Smith (Alabama), Mike Leach (Washington State), Tony Franklin (Louisiana Tech), Chad Morris (Clemson), Mike Breske (Washington State), Jon Lovett (Texas Tech), Jerry Moore (Appalachian State), David Cutcliffe (Duke), Tommy Tuberville (Texas Tech), Urban Meyer (Florida, at the time), Don James (Washington), Scott Satterfield (Appalachian State), Billy Napier (Colorado State), Gus Malzahn (Arkansas State), Shawn Elliott (South Carolina), Burton Burns (Alabama),

Danny Ford (Clemson), Eric Wolford (Youngstown State), Bob Stoops (Oklahoma), Howard Schnellenberger (Florida Atlantic), Keith Gilbertson (Washington), Jonathan Smith (Idaho), Bobby Bowden (Florida State), Steve Spurrier (South Carolina), Tommy Bowden (Clemson), Vic Koenning (North Carolina), Brad Scott (Clemson), Bill Snyder (Kansas State), and others.

Thanks to friends and associates who either helped point me in the right direction or warned me not to go in the wrong direction, including Pete Wevurski, Tony Barnhart, Bill Plaschke, the late Mike Kahn, John Clayton, Edwin Pope, and Dan Raley.

Also, not included here but of immense help in writing about Miami was the interviewing time granted me by Dwayne "The Rock" Johnson, the former Hurricanes football player, pro wrestler, and actor. Johnson talked of how Erickson challenged him in the classroom and made him present a signed form from teachers affirming he was in class that day before he would be allowed into the training room. Johnson's stories were moving and brought authenticity to the atmosphere at Miami when Erickson coached there.

1

Home of the Chokers (Late 1940s)

Following his military service Jack Swarthout could not have landed in a place more in need of what he had to offer than the community around the public high school in Hoquiam on the east end of Grays Harbor, Washington.

He was book smart and military tough, a believer in rules, punctuality, all in a place that had a historic dearth of intellectual pursuits and more than it needed of booze, broads, and quick money, usually in that approximate order. This wasn't postwar middle America from a Chamber of Commerce campaign. It was part timber boom town after everything went quiet and part poor man's Reno, all of it still living off blue-collar jobs in the mills or at the docks. Nobody would have confused Hoquiam with Mayberry. Here the deputies needed more than one bullet and had better know how to use a gun.

Swarthout was something of an odd bird, a mix of an egg-headed, voracious reader and a by-the-rules-boys war-hardened veteran and eccentric fitness freak. He was a reader of science fiction and history as a kid, firing his imagination with dreamy possibilities through books and periodicals that lifted his thoughts beyond the difficult realities of daily rural life in 1930s America. He was told, and believed with every fiber of his being, that he could be whatever he wanted to be and that a good education was the passport to get him there.

What they had in common, Swarthout the individual and Hoquiam the community, was a lack of pretense. In towns like Hoquiam and nearby Aberdeen, your smarts, sweat, and reliability took you a long way. It was a little more involved than that for Swarthout, who was enough to let his imposing presence work for him while his mental agility kept him a few steps ahead of the football players he coached and his staff. Swarthout may have asked for a little more than the community in which he got his start as an unconventional high school coach with an ability to motivate his players, but he was never a bully. It never got personal with him.

As a coach Swarthout used a compelling mix of the tangible techniques of precision blocking and tackling, packaged with concepts that were abstract for his time. He was one of the early postwar pioneers who wanted to exploit defenses with a surgical passing game instead of relying on a few simply executed pass plays designed to make an overly aggressive defense pay for stacking up to stop the run. Swarthout wanted more than a generic passing game. How much of a difference can you make when you try to do everything better than your opponent?

His military background and football experience taught him to give vigorous attention to physical discipline while his vivid imagination filled his head with abstract concepts. To Swarthout, anything was possible if you worked hard enough. The real question was, what exactly is it that you want to do?

All coaches need a key player at the right time to make their ideas relevant, and the relationship Swarthout had with his high school quarterback in Hoquiam turned out to be determinative in the development of the spread offense years later. Swarthout had no way of knowing how the passing game concepts he installed at his first coaching job would eventually evolve, but his spirit of adventure and sound technique were the seeds from which it all sprouted.

Swarthout had attended the University of Montana on athletic scholarship and played football for the Grizzlies until graduation in 1942, when the Reserve Officer Training Corps sent him off to Officer Training School and deployment around the world. By then football played a starring role in the character development and morale of the American military, which was, effectively, the greenhouse for generations of football coaching ideology.

Having emerged from elite schools in the Northeast, football spread quickly across the United States in the twentieth century and was considered to be compatible on several levels with the goals and aspirations of the armed services. Football's focus on physical fitness, attention to detail, knowing your role as part of the team—all of it reinforced and enhanced military life. Navy preflight schools established at the universities of North Carolina, Iowa, and Georgia and at Saint Mary's College in Northern California assembled football teams to compete against the top college squads in the country. The navy teams more than held their own.

How much has the world changed? In the twenty-first century troops come home from overseas in anonymity, looking for jobs, struggling to keep their families afloat. During World War II they came home to local acclaim and took positions of respect and authority, often in football.

The list of preflight football coaching veterans includes Alabama legend Paul "Bear" Bryant, Missouri's Don Faurot, and Maryland's Jim Tatum, all football coaches before, during, and after their service. Bud Wilkinson came out of an assistant coaching position at Iowa preflight and later led Oklahoma to a still-standing record of forty-seven consecutive victories.

The Army team at West Point was a national power during the war years, with talent backed up by more talent, all of it led by running backs Doc Blanchard and Glenn Davis. They dominated Heisman Trophy voting for three years, winning the prize in 1945 and '46, respectively.

Football sold the military and the military sold football to Americans, each invigorating feelings of patriotism, effort, and honor. When victorious men came back from World War II and the Korean War and got involved in college football, they married two institutions that still worked toward mutual benefit.

Many of the returning vets were former players—like Swarthout—who became coaches at small colleges or high schools after their tours of duty. They weren't just looking for jobs; many of these war veterans believed football was an instrument, maybe the best one at the time, to move young men, and the country, in a new direction. It offered the kind of pull-together teamwork talk that still occurs today, but the rewards seemed so much closer after World War II to that particular group of coaches.

Seldom have post-military opportunities had as much influence as they did at the time those enlisted men returned to classrooms and football fields after the war. They left Desolation Row and returned to the Avenue of the Americas, believing they could do anything and football was the carriage that would take them where they wanted to go.

People around the bay of Grays Harbor, Washington, ringed by the workingman's town of Hoquiam and just to the east the more "upscale" Aberdeen, were more than ready for what Swarthout had to sell. The two towns relied on a burgeoning timber industry that had frantically deconstructed the surrounding forests for profit and turned the region, in less than a century, from a pristine emerald dreamland into a smoldering pile of careless economics and witless personal vices. It was as though the region had gone on a long drunk and was finally realizing it needed to sober up and make something of itself.

If it were possible to view a time-lapse motion picture of Grays Harbor from the 1790s through the arrival of the first white settlers in the mid-1800s, the appearance of the railroad in 1895, and Swarthout's arrival roughly fifty years later, it would be a chilling piece of film to behold. The area had been inhabited by the Chehalis, Quinault, Wynoochee, and Humptulips tribes for hundreds of years prior to May 7, 1792, when Boston fur trader Robert Gray, the first white man to explore the area, crossed the bar into the dewy quiet of the pristine bay that would eventually bear his name. The Chehalis tribe named the area Ho'kweeum. Loosely translated, Hoquiam, as it was later spelled, meant "hungry for wood."

Five rivers empty into that shallow, wide bay in what became southwestern Washington State. Before long, "hungry for wood" was converted from a description of the land to a depiction of what happened when white men came in with their screaming, gas-powered saws, ripped through the tall firs, dragged them to market, and forever changed the face of the region. The railroad came right into the harbor to facilitate the retailing of the forest, and a population of hardworking, hard-drinking loggers transformed the area into something the natives never could have imagined.

In the timber business, workers could get a cash payout for each day of work in the forest and then squander it away by night in the area's bars and crowded houses of prostitution. Location was central to and almost codified the rampant debauchery. Grays Harbor became a gray area for politicians and lobbyists to the powerful. Just an hour's drive west of the state's center of political power in Olympia, it was close enough for politicians to sneak away for an afternoon or evening, yet it was far enough removed from the big-city newspapers in Seattle and Tacoma, a couple of hours' drive to the northeast, to escape their attention.

They clear-cut the land by day and partied by night, each endeavor leaving societal scars. Grays Harbor's skyline featured more than three dozen pulp, saw, shingle, and timber mills. After the community college opened in 1930, they nicknamed teams "Chokers" after the choke-setter—commonly referred to as "choker"—who was responsible for securing a cable around felled trees to be dragged out of the forest.

Smokestacks firing clouds of hot ash into the sky framed the profile of the port of Grays Harbor, so littered with years' accumulation of junk logs and unwanted wood chips that it appeared possible to walk from one end of the bay to the other across the timber debris. From mid-October through May, when morning fog, overcast skies, and drizzle were the norm rather than the exception, the place projected a foreboding panorama that provided literal heft to the color that embodied the harbor's name.

It was in this environment that someone like Jack Swarthout was both ready and welcome to any challenges.

Swarthout learned what the world looked like from a bleak adolescence on a farm in southern Washington State during the Great Depression and then came home from World War II to a culture of burgeoning prosperity and possibility. Never before and never since has a generation of Americans grown up like Swarthout's did, seeing first-hand as teenagers the economic desperations of life, then coming back from war to experience their country growing into unparalleled prosperity. All things seemed possible, especially on the football field, just like Swarthout had always believed.

Swarthout saw football's lessons as valuable to the individual player, his school, the community, and as he said many times, "to the U.S. itself." The thing that made him stand out was how he thought about winning.

Swarthout must have had an abundance of tactical genes. He was fascinated by uncommon approaches that could catch an opponent off guard and force him to scramble to make changes in the heat of the game. He became an unofficial and often unrecognized father figure of sorts to an innovative collection of northwestern football coaches who presented their own rebuttal to the coaching orthodoxy of the times. From his navy experience, Swarthout knew all about toughness, sacrifice, and determination, but he also understood that everyone else knew all about that, too. He was interested in more, namely, the great benefit of tactical thinking.

Swarthout didn't just want to beat the opposing team in a physical contest with stamina and fitness, he wanted all the advantages on his side, starting with tactics. He knew it all gets set in motion with a thought and if your concept can flummox the other guy, it was that much easier to win.

Offensive football has always been polymorphic at the strategic level, the capacity to score points being an objective that can be achieved in numerous ways by those willing to explore. Innovators are found at the edges, stressing the perfection of fundamental techniques but doing so through differing architectural designs. Swarthout was emblematic of an almost tribal band of northwestern football coaches who leaned more heavily on the thinking part of the game than most. They wanted to outthink you from the very start so you had to question every decision you made and then they wanted to beat you with execution.

To Swarthout, football was a game that improved and sharpened competitive instincts. It stressed discipline and emphasized the importance of teamwork. He felt there was an edge to be gained in the attention span of his players when he introduced a different approach or a new wrinkle to what they were already doing. In the end, he believed a kid could hop into his football vessel and, through repetition and attention to detail, learn how to become a better teammate. What he really wanted, after all of that, was to show his players how to grow up and be responsible adults.

The job teaching history and coaching at Hoquiam was, in itself, something that evidenced a kind of synchronicity. Everything Swarthout knew and believed in was emboldened by the sense of cultural chaos that blanketed Grays Harbor like a morning fog that lifts in the afternoon and returns by dawn. The oddity was that Hoquiam's mascot was the Grizzlies, the same as Swarthout's alma mater, and the bitter rival down the street in Aberdeen was the Bobcats, just as his old in-state collegiate rival, Montana State, had also been the Bobcats.

No other high schools in the state had those two nicknames. Swarthout later admitted he was looking for a high school head coaching position, preferably matched with a classroom role as a history teacher, but the clincher was coaching the Grizzlies against the hated Bobcats. It was a little football kismet at work and it just felt right.

The two schools in Hoquiam and Aberdeen still maintain the longest continuing high school rivalry west of the Mississippi River. The longer it goes, the more attention it receives, but it was an even-bigger deal back in the 1940s. There wasn't an athletic event in Grays Harbor more important than the annual Thanksgiving Day game between Hoquiam and Aberdeen.

The Aberdeen-Hoquiam game always drew capacity crowds of ten thousand to Olympic Stadium, built with local timber as a Works Progress Administration project and completed in 1938. It had the feel of a big-time facility because, when filled for games, the covered grandstand produced a booming sound out of those wooden bleachers that would make you think you were in the Rose Bowl.

Swarthout looked the part of a postwar football coach straight out of central casting. A picture of him, hands on hips in a T-shirt, sweat pants, and high-top sneakers with a tightly cropped GI flattop haircut, big shoulders, and that steely, no-nonsense, tight grin that glared out of his rugged build would have made an excellent poster for the Greatest Generation.

His approach in the classroom was somewhat didactic, strictly by the book, but his coaching, while emphasizing sound fundamentals, was forward leaning for his time in terms of its design. Swarthout believed in the three Rs, which were repetition, repetition, and repetition, principles he used to implement his version of the T formation. One of his coaching mantras was, "We're going to do it over until we get it right and then we're going to keep doing it right until we get it perfect."

He was smart enough to understand that the over-the-top drill sergeant approach was best left in the military, where it belonged, and was not suitable for the environment in which a public school educator and coach went to work each day. He wasn't an in-your-face screamer, but he surely was insistent and aggressive. He believed that in all areas of life thinking prompts action—that belief was at the core of his fascination with football tactics—so when a young man's thinking is confused, his behavior will tend to be erratic.

What Swarthout hadn't taken into account when he accepted the offer at Hoquiam was that playing sheriff would take nearly as much time as coaching. The illicit nature of daily life served to embroider his determination to invigorate the attention of his players.

There were areas in Grays Harbor that Swarthout defined as off limits for his players, imposing penalties when he got reports that lines had been crossed. He was well versed in such procedures, but Swarthout had been eager to turn the page and be a history teacher and coach, not the bad cop at Hoquiam High School. Boundaries came with the territory for football players in Grays Harbor, where Myrtle Street was the north-south dividing line that separated the two high schools. During the week leading up to the annual Thanksgiving Day game, travel was customarily restricted and players were warned against crossing Myrtle Street in the interest of avoiding altercations.

They were banned on a year-round basis from entering a three-block area called Paradise Alley, where Florence Nettleson, the area's most famous madam, had opened an upscale brothel in 1940. The prevailing notion was that without prostitution, decent women and girls would be endangered in public by bands of drunken, sex-crazed loggers. Better to let them work off their inebriated fantasies with the hookers and leave the good folk alone, or so went the theory. It was an uneasy tolerance policy that resulted in Nettleson's arrest twenty-six times from 1940 to 1951, until the community would no longer tolerate the brothels, but prostitution was going full force when Swarthout arrived. He became the football sheriff out of need.

By the time he left they might as well have named him football mayor of Grays Harbor for the influence he had over the game and the respect he had earned within the community and beyond.

Swarthout developed his forward-thinking offensive vision on the practice field behind the high school, just a few blocks removed from the livelier downtown streets. In the other direction, smokestack-pimpled hills descended into the bay, exhaling commerce into the rain and fog. Swarthout was appreciative of his small patch of turf, making it a combined refuge and training ground. There he would command the players' attention through protocol and drill them rigorously to develop the timing necessary to make the offense run as smoothly as it would have to in order to keep defenses guessing.

His observance to complete mastery of details was the systematic structure in which he built winning teams at Hoquiam. He used a T formation offense resurrected by Coach Clark Shaughnessy five years earlier at Stanford after it had been considered obsolete for decades. Swarthout developed a way to leverage a highly successful and rarely seen passing game into the offense.

Like Swarthout, Shaughnessy had an interest in history, especially military history, and he continually saw parallels between football and the movement of troops in war. A native Minnesotan, born in 1892, Shaughnessy didn't serve in the military but he studied it for most of his life and wrote many essays and magazine pieces about the strategic connections between football and war. His ideas, considered fanciful nonsense by some during his time at the University of Chicago, when the losses kept mounting up, were transformed into brilliant insights that articulated the basic structure for modern football in America when he coached the undefeated Stanford University "Wow Boys" team in 1940.

In 1940 football was still circling back on itself for ideas, but Shaughnessy's concept of the T formation was such a departure from the way most football was being played it was as though he had created the offense himself. The T formation was a nineteenth-century creation that had been deemed useless after Coach Pop Warner, with All-American Jim Thorpe at the Carlisle Indian School in Pennsylvania, popularized the single-wing formation.

The single wing and its close relative the double wing were essentially sledgehammer approaches to the game. Each relied on a tactical funneling to the point of attack of more blockers than the defense could defend against, creating a boxed canyon that linebackers had to enter but in which they could not survive the assault, outnumbered by offensive linemen and blocking backs. It was effective, it could be simply described, it worked, and it was copied in all parts of the country.

Football has always been a copycat sport, filled with coaches eager to replicate what the most successful teams are doing whether it fits their personnel or not. It's always easier for the football coach to keep his job when he explains to a school academician in charge of hiring that he is simply following the most successful formula of the day and to do this requires a certain amount of patience.

Swarthout was nothing like that, and neither was Shaughnessy, who had a revelation about the single-wing approach that led him to a reconsideration of the T formation. The act of snapping the ball 6 yards behind the line of scrimmage and then forming a blocking wall to move it 6 yards forward—as in the single wing—troubled him intellectually and tactically. It was, in effect, going backward to gather momentum toward the starting point before any actual gains of yardage could be accomplished. Better, he thought, to have the quarterback take the snap under center, turn, and hand it off to a hard-charging back who needed just a small crease in the defensive line to break through for a gain. When he imagined those holes being plugged, Shaughnessy foresaw fake handoffs or a man in motion in the backfield to draw a defender in one direction while a running play went the other way. Shaughnessy's T formation could muscle up and pound away for a short yardage gain and it could stretch a defense with deep passes.

Shaughnessy's concepts, more than anything else, catapulted football from the brutal war in the trenches it had been to what is known as modern football—a more balanced offense, with running, passing, and plenty of deception.

What Clark Shaughnessy did at Stanford in 1940 sent tremors through football orthodoxy. Sportswriters quickly took notice of how he transformed a team that had been 1-7-1 in 1939 into an undefeated champion the very next season.

He had the quarterback take the ball directly from the center's hands instead of standing a step back, as had been the practice in the original T formation. The center snap became a quicker exchange, and Shaughnessy built on that rapid start by drilling the quarterback in the proper footwork required to execute an immediate pivot and then hand the ball off to a hard-charging running back. Instead of the drive-blocking requirements of the single wing, Shaughnessy taught linemen how to "brush block," or hold their blocks just long enough to create a small opening in the line for a running lane. The idea was an aggressive snap, handoff, and just like that—bang-bang—the defense was pierced.

His teams ran drills with military precision and accounts of the schemes were told in national newspapers and magazines as his innovative ideas grew into legend with the 1940 Stanford team. Swarthout was his own man after the war, with his own views, but his love of reading and history drew him to consume Shaughnessy's theories whenever he came across them. Coaches often published writings in national publications in the 1930s and '40s, and in its October 11, 1943, issue *Time* magazine was moved to include the following review of a lengthy dissertation by Shaughnessy:

In the twelve years since Rockne's death, tall, gaunt-faced Clark Daniel Shaughnessy has indeed proved himself a top-flight coach. Last week he uncovered a second talent: military tactics. In Football in War & Peace (Jacobs Press; $1) he convincingly underscores the remarkable similarity of football strategy to tactics in warfare.

Winning touchdown of his argument is an amazing parallel between Montgomery's victory at El Alamein and a "fullback counter" run from Shaughnessy's T formation. The tactics are almost identical:

The British Eighth and Afrika Korps faced each other as on a line of scrimmage. Montgomery had the ball. His right halfback (44th Division) started the play by faking to the left and drawing off the defense. His left half (50th Division) took a fake from the quarterback, then plunged through center. Meanwhile, the fullback (United Kingdom's armored division) had started to the left. Quickly he doubled back, took the ball from the quarterback (51st Highlanders) and sliced through the right side of his line, between the defensive left end and tackle. His guard (9th Australians) blocked the defensive halfback and a historic advance had begun.

Air Power. Football's Pantelleria, says Shaughnessy, was Notre Dame's 35-to-13 upset of Army in 1913. Described by a New York paper as "a team from South Bend, Ill.," Notre Dame uncorked the historic Dorais-to-Rockne passing combination for the first convincing demonstration that air power alone can overcome land strength. From the sidelines a lightweight halfback named Dwight Eisenhower watched 13

Irish passes whistle by the hopelessly confused West Pointers. That game was the beginning of a new kind of football.

Swarthout was as caught up in the dissolution of conceptual boundaries between football and war as any of them. He spoke often about what the game taught young men, how it brought the best out of them. Even toward the end of his coaching career in 1973, when he was implicated in a scandal at the University of Montana (where he was the football coach and athletic director) that involved the misuse of government scholarship funds—*Sports Illustrated* referred to it as a "gnarled and nasty little morality play" in its April 23, 1973, issue—Swarthout was unwavering about his feelings toward the game and society.

"Athletics have so much value, not only to the university and the community but to the U.S. itself," Swarthout said in the *Sports Illustrated* article. "Football particularly. It hones the competitive instincts, it promotes discipline and cooperation. And here were these guys—G-men—treating me like I was some criminal. Still, I wanted to be honest with them; I've always been honest. Sure, we may have made some mistakes in our work-study accounting, but there was no intent to defraud Uncle Sam."

Swarthout was found not guilty of the charges that had him taking government scholarship money for players, banking it into their own account, and then "paying" them for work done, which could be a few hours a month or several hours a week.

At Hoquiam, Swarthout liked that he could pass or run with equal efficiency out of the T formation, but he was a hardcore traditionalist in that his first goal was to teach his line about blocking techniques that, properly delivered, would run an opponent into submission. His beliefs were challenged in his second year at Hoquiam when Jack Elway turned out for football and forced Swarthout to reconsider everything he thought about the game.

At the start of his junior year in high school, Elway stood six foot one, weighed 190 pounds, and could spin a football like a professional. His coach had seen taller quarterbacks, heavier ones, and faster ones, but he'd never seen one with such an advanced grasp of the game. Elway was well ahead of his time in his understanding of the importance of and his aptitude for the passing game. A knee injury in his junior year and two more by the time he got to college prematurely ended his playing career, but Jack Elway is still remembered in Grays Harbor for his high school exploits.

In 1947, after missing a few weeks with his knee injury, Elway returned for the Thanksgiving Day game and completed nine of thirteen passes for 162 yards in a 22–7 victory over Aberdeen. "You have to give Coach Swarthout and his gridders a lot of credit for their deceptive football and passing advantage with Elway," wrote Ed Stanley in the *Aberdeen World*.

In his senior season Elway completed six of ten for 139 yards in a 28–23 win over Hoquiam's archrivals and went off to Washington State College (now university) for what he hoped would be a long playing career. It wasn't. But before Jack Elway's career as a football coach was over, he would stand on the prow of a ship that changed football every bit as much as much as the arrival of Robert Gray changed forever the shallow harbor he sailed into at the end of the eighteenth century.

2

Team starts with *T*
(Late 1940s, Early 1950s)

Winning came fast and kept on coming for Jack Swarthout, regardless of the concept he was coaching. For him, it was never about latching on to one thing and living or dying with it; the beauty and the challenge was to keep evolving, ever inquisitive about what might be around the next corner. Trying new strategies fascinated Swarthout, fed his desire, and drove him to be a coach who was always tilling new ground, turning over that fresh soil, not content merely to rotate crops from one field to the next. His prize pupil picked up on that trait and made it his own.

Jack Elway was more than just a kid quarterback at Hoquiam; he had athletic gifts coaches rarely get to see. Swarthout was the chief innovator, but Elway's talent made him stretch his offensive designs more than he had ever imagined. Swarthout never guessed he'd see a high school player with Elway's natural, almost effortless ability to deliver one tight spiral after another. Just looking at the ball coming out, you'd have thought it had been launched by some Rube Goldberg mechanical throwing contraption, but Jack Elway was anything but mechanical. He was almost liquid with his footwork and his throwing motion, like some Fred Astaire in pads and helmet gliding across the stage sans Ginger Rogers.

Swarthout said coaching Elway was a breeze because the

kid was a "one-time guy," by which he meant he had to explain what he wanted only one time and Elway could make it happen over and over again. Swarthout was not the most sophisticated passing coach, but as a former receiver in college, he was aware of the basic footwork essentials he wanted to see when his quarterback dropped back to pass or turned his back to the line of scrimmage to deliver a handoff or a fake. Coming to high school coaching, Swarthout anticipated having some unrefined kids he'd have to develop to get to the point where he'd be comfortable throwing ten or fifteen passes a game.

Then he saw Elway, who, given one explanation, could replicate the footwork basics with precision every time thereafter. The ease with which he learned those basics caused Swarthout to reconsider how he would coach his version of the T formation. In a matter of a few practices, Elway had convinced him to stretch out his plan and innovate.

Swarthout's inquisitive mind crossing paths with Elway's explosive passing talent was the catalyst that moved each of them forward in their careers. Every bit as enthusiastic as his coach about exploring new ways to keep opponents off balance and out of position, Jack Elway's wheels were turning when he entered college. He just needed to learn the fundamentals of coaching.

There have always been coaching pioneers, the outliers who decided to try to do something different and discovered it works, but Swarthout and Elway are the only two coaches in America who were at the ground floor of the two modern offenses that caused the grand divergence in modern coaching strategies—the wishbone and the spread. Swarthout loved the design of the wishbone offense because it represented a smarter way to use an existing system, establishing that people, ideas, and commitment to team were the most vital components of success.

As a rule, college football coaches in the first half of the twentieth century lacked, or at least withheld, imagination, quite possibly because the popularity of the game was growing so fast they may have been more concerned with being a part of the wave of success than with trying something new and different. The single- and double-wing concepts allowed for just a few plays in a given situation, almost always running plays. Rules of the time didn't allow for plays being sent in from the sidelines, so the conservative, safety-first strategies continued until the 1930s, when the game was pried open with the forward pass, most notably at Texas Christian University in coach Dutch Meyer's offense.

He called it the Meyer spread, one slight variation removed from the double wing. It was almost the antithesis of a modern spread offense in that it was simply the old Pop Warner offense, with wingbacks—positioned more like slotbacks today—at each end of the offensive line, separated by approximately two steps from the tackles. The ball came in a direct snap to the tailback, and out of that formation Meyer created confusion with handoffs, fake handoffs, and pivots that slowed the defensive rush to the ball, because a fake handoff could also lead to a short pass to one of the wingbacks.

Meyer was ahead of the game by virtue of having been TCU's baseball coach and in that role having recruited Sammy Baugh as a pitcher. The kid had a special arm and Meyer put him in the backfield to play tailback, the designated name for the position that received the direct snap. Baugh could fling it and was deceptive in the backfield.

Baugh went on to a Hall of Fame career in the National Football League, TCU won one national and three Southwest Conference titles, and Baugh's teams in the 1930s and '40s were said to be revolutionizing the game with the pass, an arguable but often misunderstood point; even coaches often believe that what TCU did in the late '30s and '40s was a spread offense. One such coach was Georgia's Vince Dooley. When asked about his successful run in the early 1980s with the Herschel Walker–led teams, Dooley was unaware that the spread offense was in use at San Jose State University and the University of Idaho at that time and was beginning to claim victims. "I'm not sure what they were doing at Idaho when we had Herschel," Dooley said, "but if you want to talk about the spread offense and where it started, you need to start with TCU back before the war. They were running the spread way back then."

Actually, no. Dooley was misinformed, but it's an excusable misconception that helps explain why the origin of the spread has not been well understood. Semantics got in the way.

To Dutch Meyer in the 1930s, the concept he called the Meyer spread meant two slotbacks lined up on the outside hip of the tackle at either end of the line of scrimmage. By the time Dooley was hearing about spread offenses fifty years later the term was used more literally, with up to five intended receivers, backs, tight ends, and wide receivers stretched out across the field, literally forcing defenses to spread out. While Dutch Meyer's TCU teams did open up a semblance of a controlled, short passing game, the distinction in what the Horned Frogs were doing made all the difference.

In its magical season of 1938, when TCU was 11-0 and won the mythical national championship, the Meyer spread was in full bloom. Davey O'Brien threw for 1,457 yards that season, including nineteen touchdowns and just four interceptions. He threw a total of 194 passes, 17.6 a game, out of the Meyer spread, which was not really a spread by any definition, and the seventeen to eighteen passes a game didn't exactly fill the air with footballs.

However, in the 1930s and '40s the college game was so defined by power running, it made TCU look like a passing circus by comparison and the name Meyer applied to his offense could cause one to believe it had something to do with the spread offense Jack Elway would eventually introduce to college football thirty years later. It's preposterous that Meyer's offense was any sort of antecedent to the spread, but myths have a way of working like that. Had global tensions not been ramping up the way they were, Meyer's short, safe passing game might have been more popular, but the war years focused attention even more on power football.

Meyer's offense was surely creating a buzz, but it turned out it was Shaughnessy, if anyone in particular, who could be said to have truly changed conventional thought about the forward pass when he went to Stanford in 1940.

Clark Shaughnessy had been the coach at the University of Chicago for Jay Berwanger, the initial winner of what came to be known as the Heisman Trophy. Because of Berwanger's passing skills, Shaughnessy imagined a revamped T formation, with the quarterback taking the snap under center and dropping back to hand off or pass, but his talent was so thin at Chicago he never put it to use. Instead, Shaughnessy had the ear of Chicago Bears owner and coach George Halas.

Professional football was almost an afterthought in those prewar years; college football was taking over almost from coast to coast. Baseball was big but confined to the major cities in the East, while in the South and Midwest and on the West Coast, college football was king.

Shaughnessy considered himself a professor of football; his intellectual cravings for the game fed his imagination night and day. He became a Halas confidant and the Bears' coach used many of his concepts in the implementation of the T formation in pro football, probably the single most influential factor in making the game more appealing to the public.

Much derision followed his hiring in 1940 at Stanford, as Shaughnessy had been 17-34-1 at the University of Chicago—the school dropped football when he left—including 4-18-1 in his last three seasons. At Chicago, he was a visionary thinker caught in a place that was reconsidering its interest in football. Shaughnessy had replaced the legendary Amos Alonzo Stagg, but school president Robert Hutchins had raised academic standards at the time of the new hire—limiting the pool of recruits—and told Shaughnessy the school would be known for academics, not athletics. He really didn't have a chance at Chicago, but Shaughnessy's desire to coach burned red hot, and when the time came, he enthusiastically accepted the Stanford job.

Some hire for Stanford, they thought, until his first year, when he coached the team to an undefeated season and a 21–13 win over Nebraska in the Rose Bowl. Leading them on the field was a five-foot-nine, left-handed quarterback named Frankie Albert who was unremarkable in the single wing but became a two-time All-American for Shaughnessy in the T formation.

Albert was a magician with the ball. He could hide it on his hip and run away from the flow of the offense untouched on one play, then deftly hand it off to a back on the next play and make it appear as though he still had the ball. When he threw downfield, receivers were often wide open because of Albert's ball-handling abilities.

More than TCU's Meyer and his "spread" offense, it was Shaughnessy's T formation that began to open the eyes of coaches. Shaughnessy invented a deceptive approach to what had been considered an almost hopelessly conservative, one-dimensional, thud-into-the-line offense. At Stanford he took great advantage of a new twist, the man in motion. His little quarterback was good on the move and Stanford opponents found themselves grasping for answers when a back or an end would be sent in motion one way and the flow of the play would go the other way.

It was among the first indications in major college football that the way the game had been played was not the way it would be played in the future. The game was on the move, literally.

Swarthout liked Shaughnessy's approach and was running the T formation at Hoquiam the year before Elway turned out, but if he had been using a different offense, this kid would have made him innovate. "Swarthout was the leader, the general, the strategist," said Bob Beers, who played for Swarthout in college. "He was very, very smart and he instilled in us a pride and sense of purpose for what we were doing that brought us together as a team, as a family, really. He knew what he was talking about and we all understood that, we just didn't want to let him down."

Coaching the T formation wasn't extremely unusual, but the way Swarthout coached it and the quarterback he had to run it set those Hoquiam teams apart. Braced with an almost evangelical zeal, Swarthout developed in his players the kind of orderly self-control that kept his boys out of the bars and flophouses and molded them into a winning team.

It worked with Elway, though he was one whose parents had him pointed in that direction anyway. His father, a plumber, prodded Jack toward college. In a single day, he might repair a sink line in an upscale home on the hill, unclog a toilet in a whorehouse, or investigate a banging pipe in a shingle mill. What he saw convinced him that he wanted something better for his son, something only a college education could provide. Elway was one of the better students in school and showed a drive to do things with his life. He talked about working in football even when he was in high school.

Bob Klock, a Hoquiam teammate who later worked for Elway as an assistant coach, saw a side of him few knew. "He was a helluva quarterback," Klock said, "everybody knew that, but what set him apart was his mind. Jack was very bright, very knowledgeable about football almost from the start; he understood the important parts of the game before most of us caught on, he was a very quick learner, and he was always tinkering, trying new and different things. He and Swarthout were perfect for each other and they knew it."

The world may well have seen Jack Elway become a standout professional quarterback, were it not for his torn-up knees. Bad knees aside, ironically enough, for a quarterback who knew how to pass, Elway couldn't have picked a worse place to further his football education. He enrolled at Washington State.

3

High School Football (Early 1950s)

Conditions had changed for the better in America by 1950, when blue-collar manufacturing sent the U.S. brand around the world and an average Joe could make a decent enough living to afford a house and a car and still send a kid to college. The newfound might of the nation was busting out all over, but the modernization of American life had managed to skip college football, which was still being conducted in a strategic maze that benefited the most well-heeled programs and left little for those that lacked the tradition and marketing appeal that lured recruits to big schools.

Many returning soldiers found welcome signs at colleges and universities where coaches were well-known war veterans who could forge an immediate connection with them. Other returning vets, like Robert "Pinky" Erickson, wanted to go home and find a high school where they could put what they had learned into practice. In Erickson's case, staying warm was part of the appeal in returning to the Northwest; a larger part was exploring the meaning of the lessons he had absorbed in his time with the 201st Infantry in Adak, Alaska, a desolate, inhospitable outpost in the Aleutian Islands. Erickson spent nearly two years there, in what was later called the "Forgotten Theater" of the war. It was an area seen as a potential Japanese entry point to North

America, but twenty days of fighting by the 201st the year before Erickson arrived had taken back the island and he and his company saw no combat in their time there. Nonetheless, or maybe because of relatively expansive opportunities for reflective solitude, he believed what he experienced there changed the way he understood the world.

Erickson and almost all World War II soldiers participated in a strategic-training approach called small-group cohesion that the army used with great success for a time in the 1940s and early 1950s. The concept, incorporated around the world by numerous fighting forces in various governmental systems, involves recognition of the human element in war and of the need to strengthen force by building bonds between individuals, thereby sustaining commitment to the unit and the mission. Small-group cohesion captured the idea of how great accomplishments can be achieved in groups when the relative importance of individual recognition is diminished.

No surprise that the small-group belief structure would take over college football after the war, implemented by returning veterans who entered the coaching profession. Among the coaches who used principles of small-group cohesion in building their teams during the post–World War II years are Bear Bryant, with his legendary "Junction Boys" teams at Texas A&M and his later teams at Alabama, and Bud Wilkinson at Oklahoma.

In World War II troops were brought together in boot camp and stayed together through basic training and throughout their tours of duty around the world. They learned how do things "the army way," from making beds and shining boots to engaging the enemy, but what they really learned, what Erickson carried with him the rest of his days, was the value of individual accountability, the importance of trusting one another, and the necessity of finding ways of working together to achieve goals. Accountability, sacrifice, and trust have been the building blocks of football for the past seventy years, replacing the hierarchal, top-down, boilerplate structure that established the early brutality of college football. Pinky Erickson—so nicknamed because of his fair skin and ginger hair (one of the older kids down the block was Red, another, a year older, was Rusty)—absorbed those lessons naturally in Adak. Small-group cohesion was an extension of his neighborhood back home.

His parents, Oscar, a shingle weaver in a lumber mill outside of Everett, Washington, and Erma, a store clerk, raised him with the specific intent of directing him toward a career in public education. They had carved out a meaningful existence for their family through the combined efforts of dangerous work in the mills and the routine of working a cash register in a general store. They wanted something better for their son.

Pinky said his mother often reminded him, "Children will always learn, so get a good education and teach them something better than we were taught." Oscar's Catholic parents had fled religious persecution in Sweden in the mid-1800s, drawn to the United States by the Homestead Act. The freedom Pinky Erickson's parents found in their new country was reflected in their feelings toward other races and religions. They would not abide discrimination in any form, having felt its suffocating grip in Sweden. Oscar and Erma passed those values on to Pinky and his older brother by fourteen years, Chuck.

In Everett the Ericksons were part of a community where people relied on each other, shared transportation and food, and cared for each other's children when necessary. Pinky brought a formalized, adult version of his childhood understanding of community to his life in the army. He was fascinated by the feeling that he was part of something bigger than he had ever known and also by the realization that everyone was tasked to play a necessary role.

In Adak his superiors laid out exacting duties that carried the message that each soldier was a vital link in the chain of command. From the first day he arrived in Alaska, Erickson's concept of group cohesion was connected to football. A football talisman guided the men of Adak in the 201st. Before Erickson arrived, Col. John Hamilton had an operations sergeant design a logo of a Kodiak bear to symbolize the spirit of the 201st. The bear stood upright and bore a menacing expression. In its right paw, drawn back, poised to be launched, sat an artillery shell, as if the bear were a quarterback spotting a receiver deep in the end zone. These bastards meant to fight.

Erickson brought that confidence back with him to Ferndale, an hour's drive north of his hometown, Everett, but more central to his coaching was the belief he had in the effects of small-group cohesion. He had seen top-down leadership with its screaming and demands and he had also seen what happens when lines of communication are opened and people are called to work together, as in the military, as in football. It wasn't about the violence of war; Pinky Erickson didn't know about that. It was about the power of the group, a concept that was lodged in his consciousness.

Based on his experience with troops that were able to maximize their capabilities only when they worked together, Erickson built a football-coaching career on the principle of bringing everyone to the party. Nothing was more important to him than teammates building bonds of trust with each other through shared accountability. That's where the confidence came from: players working together and expecting mental and physical effort at the highest levels.

Erickson believed if he could build those levels of trust he could be a successful football coach. Even if his team wasn't successful, they would at least know that it was because a better team had beaten them and not because they weren't ready to make the commitment required to prepare.

The high school coaching careers of Jack Elway and Pinky Erickson began percolating purposefully in the early 1950s in northwestern Washington, just when Jack Swarthout's reputation was about to take him to a bigger stage.

At Ferndale, Erickson, a history teacher, became a small-town celebrity almost overnight when his Golden Eagles began winning games. People couldn't understand why it was that, while he took the same kind of kids they had always had, instead of being not quite good enough, Erickson's teams were just good enough to win most of the time. When they finally beat Bellingham, the much larger school in the college town a few miles south, Pinky Erickson was a hero.

He was the grand marshal in a Labor Day parade, he spoke to every civic group he could, and along the way he took particular note of the Lummi Nation people whose tribal lands were just west of the high school. The Lummi people were always present at Golden Eagle games. Erickson became a hero to the Lummi community as well when a Lummi kid didn't show up to school one day in the winter. The school called and a voice at the other end said the boy left for school like always, so at the end of the day, Erickson went looking, just as the sun was going down. He found the boy in a makeshift lean-to, shivering, afraid to go home, where his mom and dad had had a big fight the night before.

Saturday mornings in the fall Pinky would take Dennis, his first-born child and only son, for a drive to Bellingham, where they would pick up game film from the night before. Erickson may have been the first high school coach in the state to regularly use film as a way to evaluate his team's games. He had a friend from Western Washington University who had been studying film and agreed to try capturing the games on Friday night fields under less than ideal lighting conditions. The films were grainy, parts were useless, but they went through the visible stuff over and over again. By the time father and son got back home, a few assistant coaches and volunteer coaches would have arrived, Mary Erickson would have tacked a sheet to the living room wall, and they would sprawl out along the floor to see what they could learn.

Without realizing it, young Dennis Erickson was getting a million-dollar education in football. He learned offensive line blocking techniques and would practice them in slow motion with one of the coaches — "That's it, get down low like that and you control that guy" — while picking up on terms like *protection schemes* and the difference between two deep and three deep safeties.

By the time he was six years old, Dennis knew he wanted to be like his dad, the most popular guy in town. His friends had fathers who were farmers, truck drivers, and fishermen, there were lots of those in Ferndale, but there was only one football coach, and everybody wanted to know more about him.

Had he been born ten years later, it is altogether possible that what we know about big-time quarterbacks might be altered with a significant addition named Jack Elway.

His son John is in the Pro Football Hall of Fame, and few connoisseurs of the game who saw John play would say they ever saw a quarterback with a better arm or a more finely tuned delivery. That may be because those people never saw John's father play football. "I don't think I ever watched John

Elway play on TV or in person with Jack Swarthout when he didn't say, 'His old man threw just like that,'" said Bob Beers, a member of the first Montana team that Swarthout coached in 1967. "If he hadn't torn up his knee, he wouldn't have been coaching all those years."

Jack Elway's time in Pullman was not part of the glory years at Washington State, and the school surely was not the most desirable place for a passing quarterback under Coach Forest Evashevski, still trying to make something out of the old single-wing, direct-snap offense he had played in at Michigan for Coach Fritz Crisler. It was an offense that Elway realized was outdated by the offense he had played in for Swarthout at Hoquiam High. Had he not been injured, Elway would have been mostly wasted in Evashevski's offense, but a second knee injury as a freshman ended his playing career anyway.

When he left Washington State after two years for the University of Iowa, Evashevski said that he had always believed the Big 10 Conference was where the best college football was played and he had always dreamed of coaching there. He never would have believed that nearly thirty years later Elway would be at ground zero for an offense that would turn college football inside out, even in the Big 10, where the insurrection would be led by Joe Tiller, an Elway protégé.

After his injuries forced him from the team, Elway played a little flag football in a fraternity league in Pullman in which he assumed roles of both a player and an unofficial coach. He played quarterback, doing little more than receiving the snap in what would later be known as a shotgun formation, but he revealed his forward thinking even before his coaching career began. Elway would split players out wide on those flag teams, move a back in motion, and then confuse the defense more by having the back move into a pass pattern on the same side with an end.

It seems basic by modern standards, but few teams even put players in presnap motion back then. Elway would take the snap, drop back, and fling it all day, truly ahead of his time, not just by a little bit, but by a decade or more. Had he not been injured, Jack Elway had the kind of knowledge of the game combined with rare physical gifts that would have been noticed by professional scouts, even in a restricted offense.

Instead, Elway went straight into coaching. After graduating high on the dean's list at Washington State he applied for teaching and coaching jobs all over the state. He could have done a lot worse than where he landed, at Port Angeles High School, 150 miles north of Hoquiam, where the land was fat with timber, the water in the Strait of Juan de Fuca thick with fish, all around a town where the timber and fishing industries converged and crackled with commercial energy that wouldn't slow down for another decade.

By the time he got to Port Angeles as the head baseball coach and assistant basketball coach in 1953, Elway—who taught biology and economics while working on his master's degree at Washington State in the summer—was adept at deconstructing offensive and defensive designs and breaking them into their component parts to examine their structural flaws and benefits. In his second year he continued as the baseball coach and added the role of basketball coach. By the fall of 1956 he had his master's and was named assistant football coach as well as serving as head coach in the other two sports.

In 1958 Elway was named head coach in football. He initially kept his roles as head coach in basketball and baseball but dropped them in his third season to focus on running the football team. His Port Angeles teams were historic for their innovation and success. The Roughriders were 6-0 in league play and 7-2 overall his first year, followed by records of 6-0 (8-1) and 4-2 (7-3) before he left to assume the football coaching position back home at Grays Harbor Community College. In all, Elway's three teams were 16-2 in league play and 22-6 overall, but the numbers don't tell the whole story. He was winning football games, but more important in the long run, he was looking for ways out of the dogmatic coaching maze that dominated football thought.

"Jack was always looking to throw the ball, which I loved," said Gary Gagnon, who played wide receiver for Elway at Port Angeles before moving on to a college career as a player and coach at Washington State and then becoming a respected coach at Evergreen High School, between Seattle and Tacoma. "He was so innovative with the stuff he had the quarterback do; we were reverse pivoting the quarterback and having him get away from the line and hiding the ball so the defense couldn't see it. Army had that 'Lonesome End' formation with Bill Carpenter in 1959 and we were doing the same thing, the same year. I have no idea where he found out about it, but my memory is that we were doing it before I even heard about Army doing it."

Elway also had an unconventional approach to communication with his players. Once, after a difficult game on the road at Forks, near the tip of the Olympic Peninsula, Elway heard an assistant coach, Dee Hawkes, chewing out players for not executing techniques "his way." While Hawkes showered, Elway reminded him that it wasn't the assistant coach's team, it wasn't his way of doing things, that they were all in it together, it was "our team," not his team. Elway asked if he got it, and Hawkes responded apologetically, saying it wouldn't happen again. Elway said that was good, telling him that he needed to think about what he was saying before he spoke. With that, Elway turned off the hot water and walked out as Hawkes stood naked under a cold stream of water.

In the 1950s Elway was thinking about spreading out defenses while specializing in acts of deception with the quarterback's ball handling as a way of keeping the defense from pursuing the flow of the play. Imbued in the concepts of small-group cohesion through the teachings of Jack Swarthout, Elway would tell his team he had a certain number of things he wanted to accomplish in practice and if everyone was attentive and worked hard, they wouldn't be kept late.

"He told me he had torn up his knee at WSU when Evashevski was running them into the ground with drills at the end of practice one time," Gagnon recalled. "Evashevski said, 'One more time,' and Jack said he was more intent on staying in the front of the drill than he was on his footwork and he rushed through a cut, his cleat got caught, and his knee went out.

"When I coached," Gagnon said, "Jack always said, 'Don't ever say one more time when you know they've had enough.'"

As Jack Elway and Pinky Erickson were building high school coaching reputations in the state of Washington and sharing ideas at coaching seminars in the off-season, Jack Swarthout's reputation was expanding beyond high school. A decade earlier, Swarthout had some ideas he was passionate about that he believed could help teams win football games. Now it was 1956 and he was in major college football at the University of Washington, on a staff with a head coach everyone knew was going places.

4

Big-Time College Football
(Mid to Late 1950s)

There exists not a single self-respecting fan of the grand traditions of the University of Alabama football program who does not nod with a knowing smile when asked about the role played by the University of Washington in Crimson Tide mythology. Mythology, because some of the memories Alabama faithful hold true to their heart as fact can really be seen to contain only a few slender threads of truth wrapped inside layers of mystique.

Among the most treasured artifacts of Alabama history are the national championships won by the school, starting with the 1925 Rose Bowl. In the first half of the twentieth century, all manner of groups and individuals named teams as national champions of college football, and anytime a group, obscure or well-known, mentioned the Tide, the title was taken seriously. Some of the "championships" Alabama won on the football field may be questionable, but the first one, the one they say legitimized football in the South, should always count.

Southern college football originally wasn't taken seriously by observers and fans because the early champions were from the Northeast, where the game originated, at places like Princeton, Yale, Rutgers, and Pennsylvania. That recognition was wrested away convincingly by Coach Gil Dobie at Washington when the Huskies went 59-0-3 over a nine-year stretch from 1908 to 1916, a standard that has never been duplicated.

Those perfect seasons in Seattle established the brand of college football on the West Coast, and the Huskies may have still been living on some of that past success when they initially declined the Rose Bowl invitation after the 1925 season. They had lost only once the year before, and in '25 Washington opened with a 108–0 victory over Willamette. After four games they had outscored opponents 253–10 on the way to a 10-0-1 record.

Play another game? Why? College football considered its season officially over prior to the bowl games. Voting on national champions was always conducted before the bowl season until 1968. The original concept of the Rose Bowl was to be an exhibition game to fill out the day following the main event, the Rose Parade.

Eventually Washington reconsidered, after Dartmouth and Tulane, coached by Clark Shaughnessy (prior to his days at Chicago and Stanford), passed on the opportunity. Alabama was eager, supported by a telegram from the governor to Rose Bowl officials, beseeching them to invite the Tide, which was eventually selected to challenge Washington.

The Huskies' great running back George Wilson, probably the player of the year nationally in 1925, scored early. Washington took the lead but Wilson was hit hard in the ribs and missed the second and third quarters. He came back in the fourth, but too late to prevent a 20–19 Alabama victory that made football king in the South. And for Washington, it was the beginning of the end of their successful run, a decline that would last for about twenty-five years.

By the time the war ended Washington's football boosters were hungry to get back in the game—at the top. The desire to get into the national spotlight was satisfied through the play of All-American running back Hugh McElhenny and quarterback Don Heinrich in the early 1950s. Those two teamed with Jack Elway's favorite Hoquiam High School receiver, Bill Early, to lift the Huskies to national prominence. The administration, athletic department and coaching staff liked the warm glow of attention and they wanted more.

None of the architects of that turn-of-the-century Husky success was around in the late 1940s and early 1950s when school leaders mapped out a plan to return Washington to the college football summit. Much of it was connected to creating interest nationally by scheduling games against prominent Midwestern teams, including Notre Dame and Minnesota. It looked good on paper but came apart on the field when the Huskies lost divisive home-and-home games to Notre Dame by a combined 73–7 and lost the first three against the Golden Gophers.

Worse, the great years with McElhenny and Heinrich were blemished by a slush-fund scandal that cost Coach John Cherberg his job and placed the Huskies on probation for two years. McElhenny later famously said that his wife's job through the slush-fund organization brought them about $10,000 in his last two years at the school, so there was some truth in his line that he took a pay cut for his $7,000 contract with the San Francisco 49ers.

Washington was looking to recover from NCAA sanctions and build a physically tough team when it hired a young Oklahoman named Darrell Royal in 1956 to get the Huskies pointed in the right direction. Royal had a bit of a vagabond reputation, having held assistant jobs at three different schools in successive years, taken a head coaching position in the Canadian Football League for a year, and then gone to Mississippi State for two years before accepting the job offer in Seattle.

Royal resolved to build the Huskies into a winning program by solidifying the local recruiting base. If the state produced two or twenty major college football players in a given year, he wanted them all, so he sought inside advice from the area's top coaches. His advisors included Swarthout, who became a close confidant of Royal's after he was hired to coach running backs and head up the recruiting efforts.

Royal could manage only a 5-5 record that first year, but his reputation was such that he was wanted in Texas. When the offer came from Austin, Royal jumped at it, replacing Ed Price at the end of a 1-9 season. He convinced Swarthout to join him on his Longhorns' staff and it was a good marriage for a decade. After the 1966 season Montana called Swarthout back to his alma mater to be the Grizzlies' head coach. He may have arrived in Montana shortly after the season, but he was far from done with Texas and experimentation.

While his mentor was drilling into the details of the running game at Washington, then at Texas for Darrell Royal, Jack Elway was involved in similar investigation of the passing game at Port Angeles High School.

Elway's self-discovered belief was that you had to work your ass off searching for clues to those little things that, done consistently well, came together to form one big thing, winning. Repetition would eventually provide a spark of inspiration.

"We would spend an incredible amount of time on little things done right," said Gary Gagnon.

We had one play where the quarterback would reverse pivot — away from the flow — fake a handoff, and hide the ball on his hip at this certain angle Jack wanted and the other back would take it from him, almost like a Statue of Liberty play, but it was incredibly effective. Jack would sit in a chair on the defensive side of the ball—he'd move the chair all around and watch—and we would run that play over and over, with him making these little tweaks each time. He wanted the footwork absolutely precise and the angle the quarterback stood at just so, until he was satisfied that you couldn't see the ball from any of those positions where he would sit.

I didn't realize at the time that he was concocting all these other plays to use as window dressing for that play. We would use it maybe two or three times a game, but he spent the whole game setting it up like a sucker punch. Another thing he did that I didn't hear about until the '70s was he would script plays, usually seven or eight of them that we'd take into the game. We had lots of motion and we passed maybe fifteen to twenty times a game, when nobody was doing that. Most teams passed five or six times but we mixed it up real good, I mean we had great confidence as a team because we knew the defense never knew what was coming.

Elway's innovative concepts were only part of his success, according to those who played for him. They will tell you that the belief he instilled in his teams and his competitive fire would have made any team successful. "I don't know if I was ever around a more competitive guy, certainly not when I was growing up," Gagnon said. "He coached basketball and in the off-season he would have the gym open before school in the morning. He loved to play us one on one, and I mean, it was all you could do to not take a swing at him. If he had the ball, he would step on your foot and drive by you, he'd trip you, push you, he always had a hand on you and he'd go up for a rebound with forearm on your shoulder so you couldn't jump. He was absolutely relentless."

Those lessons were central to an understanding Elway generated within his teams. "He always said the most important thing about a football team was the chemistry and the relationships that are developed between the players and the coaches," said Bob Beers, who played at Montana when Elway was an assistant there on Jack Swarthout's staff in the late 1960s. "He said once you get that chemistry going, you're going to have a good football team."

Elway had learned about that team-building aspect of the game when he played for Swarthout, but he also was a natural for developing such chemistry. It was part of his personality.

"First, he loved to laugh," said Bob Klock, Elway's top assistant at Port Angeles. "For as serious as he was about the game, about his offensive concepts, Jack knew it was a game and he knew it had to be fun in order for teams to be successful. And let's face it—he was the kind of guy you knew you could talk to, he exuded that."

Elway liked his occasional social drink and he was a chain smoker. But he had a quick wit and a sharp mind you couldn't forget. He had no interest in dressing up for anybody and generally looked like a guy who didn't get enough rest and frequently slept in his clothes. He was characterized by a messy desk, a cluttered office, wrinkled sport coats, and messy cars you had to see to believe. His cars got washed only when it rained and Elway had the bad habit of dumping an astray full of cigarette butts on the passenger-side floor. When you accepted a ride from him, you would have to lift your feet up, or else they would fall into a pile of butts rising six inches off the floorboard.

Ten years before *The Odd Couple* was a Broadway play in 1965 and twenty years before Jack Klugman and Tony Randall played the roles on television, Jack Elway and Bob Klock were that couple as high school coaches in Port Angeles. Klock was meticulously organized, neat in appearance, and always taking notes at the many coaching clinics they would attend in the Northwest. Elway was the rumpled guy who would poke fun at Klock and others if he thought they might be wearing a new shirt. He not only enjoyed his wrinkled clothes, he taunted others for being neat, even as he realized social norms had to be maintained, which he did, at the most minimal level.

Elway always had a clip-on tie handy when situations like teaching his biology class called for one, and he kept himself from looking like a complete rube by hooking a rubber band around his lower shirt button and onto his belt so the shirt wouldn't come untucked. Low as they may have been, you could say he had his standards.

Elway taught his quarterbacks timing that was syncopated to the dance-like rhythm of their drop backs. He had about a three-second window of operation for his quarterback to survey the defense, pick out a receiver, and either deliver the ball, throw it away, or take a safe run. He didn't want the quarterback counting because he thought that was distracting. Instead, the step-back rhythm inculcated a kind of unconscious clock Elway demanded. He wanted his quarterback sensing rather than consciously thinking about the right time to throw, a result of the practiced discipline of repetition he had learned in high school, playing for Swarthout.

The understanding that a confident team will always take an edge into a game over a team that lacks confidence came from his experience on those Hoquiam teams. Elway felt it so deeply that he made it an inviolable rule for any team he coached. Players would always be held personally accountable within the team and that pact would unavoidably build trust and confidence by putting the team first in all things, at all times, in every circumstance.

Dee Hawkes, the young coach who had Elway turn cold

water on his approach earlier in his career, became a trusted sidekick who attributed his motivation to make coaching football a career to his time with Elway. After the shower incident, he attended virtually every clinic Elway conducted with other coaches the rest of his time at Port Angeles. Elway would have Hawkes sit in the one of the first few rows and take voluminous notes on everything that was said, while Elway would head for the bar, usually for a chat with another coach. He was always being asked to speak, but Elway was a poor public speaker. He knew what he wanted for his team, he knew how to deliver that message, but he wasn't enthused about speaking before groups. Instead he would dig information out of a couple of coaches and combine it with what Hawkes heard to get the most out of the clinics.

From a technical standpoint, Elway believed winning was hidden in the way you ran drills, how you eliminated wasted time in practice, how you found ways to let kids have fun at something you could win with; it was all those things and more, but at the core of the job was this constant examination and ongoing reconstruction of the process. And yes, repetition.

Mostly it was about the gift Elway had for processing information. A lot of coaches are spellbinding speakers who could make more money in sales if only football weren't so seductive, all wrapped up in ego, bravado, and winning. The number of former football coaches who went on to better-paying jobs in the insurance or car sales business is extensive. Some of them became motivational speakers and joined corporate firms that, for a price, imparted winning wisdom in business seminars. To hear them talk, they were all champions, but of course, had they been, they would have never left coaching. Most of them, truth be told, were almost-good coaches who talked the game better than they could coach it. Not all of them listened as well as Elway, so it sort of balanced out in the end. Elway had an accelerated capacity to hear isolated messages in someone else's words that applied to his own coaching.

In those years at Port Angeles Elway's Roughriders were so successful that the 1958 team was hailed as the greatest the school ever produced. Football historians will note another contribution Elway made in that time: fathering John, born with his twin sister, Jana, in 1960, eighteen months after the birth of Elway's oldest daughter, Lee Ann. A fifty-year reunion of the 1958 Port Angeles High School team featured an autographed football by John Elway that was enshrined in the school's trophy case following a banquet attended by two-dozen members of the team.

It was only a matter of time until Jack Elway moved up in the coaching ranks, and that time came the year after John and Jana were born. In 1961 Elway was hired, with Swarthout's recommendation, as the football coach back home at Grays Harbor Community College. Over the course of six years there Elway produced teams with a combined 32-17-2 record, three of them achieving national rankings in 1963–65.

His son would become a Hall of Fame player, one of the greatest to ever play quarterback in the NFL and one of the first in America to play his entire high school career in a spread offense.

Pinky Erickson was the first football coach at Cascade, a high school that opened in Everett, Washington, in 1960. Erickson's high school pal Norm Lowery, a basketball coach, had helped him land a teaching job at Ferndale, and Lowery also helped him in Everett. When the new school was mentioned, Lowery dropped Erickson's name. In 1959 Erickson was added to the football coaching staff at Everett as a special assistant to Bill Dunn and the next year he became the coach at Cascade when the school first opened its doors.

What hadn't been determined at the time of the move were the precise boundaries of the redesigned school district. Everyone thought it was odd when the house the Ericksons bought happened to be the one next door to Dunn. The two rivals were neighbors. It got stranger yet when the school boundaries were set to follow the property line between the two houses. The Erickson family discovered they were in the Everett district, while the Dunns' home was in the Cascade district. That meant Dennis Erickson would play for Everett and be coached by Dunn, his next-door neighbor, competing against his father, the Cascade coach. "We just didn't talk about it," Dennis said. "On game day we would eat together and it just wasn't a topic, we just knew not to go there."

In grade school, then later in junior high and high school in Everett, Dennis Erickson was a popular kid. He was the point guard of the basketball team that played in the state finals and he quarterbacked the football team that was one of the best in the state in a time before statewide playoffs. He got good grades and was the class president, but all of it started on the floor of the living room on Saturday mornings. His mother, Mary, and sisters, Christy, Julie, and Nancy, would make sandwiches and snacks and the Cascade coaches would spend the late morning and all afternoon looking for ways to improve the team. Other kids had dads who made more money, but they didn't ride in parades like Erickson's dad, they didn't walk the sidelines on those Friday nights in Whatcom County when it seemed the whole community turned out to watch the Golden Eagles.

Dennis's father's influence on him was thorough. The kid was marinated in football from the time Mary first carried him to a game in a baby blanket on a Friday night. He was never pushed toward the game, he was drawn to it by his father's occupation, and the more he learned, the more he wanted to know.

The Ericksons quickly became part of their new community in Everett. Pinky worked with Bill Dunn and the Everett High School team while Cascade was being finished and Dennis attended South Everett Junior High School, where he was rapidly absorbed into the fabric of the teenage jock community. Dennis played with boys at both schools, with kids like Mike Price, a North Junior High student whose father was the coach at Everett Community College, and with kids from the wider area, such as Keith Gilbertson from nearby Snohomish. Gilbertson's father, yet another coach, supervised the Everett Stadium field over the summer months when it was open for youth league play.

By the time Dennis Erickson was beginning to fill out physically as a sophomore in high school, Price was the quarterback of the team. Erickson was a kind of hybrid running back and slotback, an aggressive, smart player who was too good to keep off the field even though he hadn't really settled in at a position. The following summer Price developed a staph infection that caused him to miss the first few weeks of fall practice. It was during that time that Dunn moved Erickson in at quarterback. Price came back to start the season, but he wasn't physically fit because of his illness, and after three games Erickson was the starting quarterback of the Everett Seagulls.

Dunn's offense was a derivative of the multiple-option approach that was trendy through the country in the 1960s and '70s. It required a quarterback tough enough to take the ball and run when he spotted a defensive vulnerability and smart enough to hand it off, toss it to a trailing running back, or throw it to a receiver or tight end when those opportunities presented themselves, qualities at which Erickson excelled from all his hours of film study.

By the time he got to high school, Erickson knew defensive tendencies without having to think about them. When he went down the line with the ball, he knew by their footwork and positioning whether defenders were coming at him or staying back to protect. His coaches thought of him as a natural, but it was more a case of natural progression after almost ten years of watching film with his father's coaching staffs.

He was also involved in more traditional forms of leadership within the school structure. Erickson's senior-class picture in the school yearbook, showing him smiling in a sport jacket and narrow tie along with his burr-headed haircut, is accompanied by a lengthy list of involvements: Boys Club president, ushers' cochairman, executive committee of student council, executive board member of the representative assembly, student leadership conference member, and letterman in track (pole vault, two years), basketball, and football (three years each, team captain of each as senior).

As a sophomore he quarterbacked the football team to an unbeaten record in six games. In his junior and senior seasons Erickson led the Seagulls to 9-1 records each year, winning two of three games against his dad's team at Cascade. His leadership was so well known that Montana State coach Jim Sweeney offered him a scholarship without ever seeing him play football in person. Sweeney knew Everett coach Bill Dunn, and he knew the player's father, Pinky Erickson, even better from coaching seminars and clinics and the inescapable fact that the two of them couldn't stop talking and would wear each other out whenever they were together.

Although he never saw Dennis Erickson play football in high school, Sweeney had seen some film that piqued his interest. He also saw the kid play as point guard for Everett's basketball team in the championship game of the state tournament, in which the underdog Everett Seagulls nearly upset favored Garfield, which featured three players who went on to play Division I college basketball. Sweeney watched Erickson dish out a state tournament record fourteen assists, most of them to Lou Hobson, an African American teammate who was Erickson's closest non-football-playing friend in high school and also lived with the Erickson family. Hobson's parents had marital issues—one lived in Everett, one in Seattle—and for the better part of two years, Hobson lived with the Erickson family, sharing a room upstairs with Dennis.

It was in the stands at the University of Washington's Hec Edmundson Pavilion the night of the State Championship game that Sweeney decided to offer Erickson a scholarship. "I wanted to see him play football, but I didn't need to," Sweeney said. "I knew he was a leader from watching him play basketball. On the floor he was absolutely expressionless, but he ran the team. What I remember was watching during timeouts on the sideline: Dennis would be in the middle of the circle, taking over, demanding, fist-pumping, encouraging. I loved that about him and that's basically what convinced me I wanted him on my football team."

At Montana State Erickson forged a rare relationship with Sweeney that endured until Sweeney's death in 2013, which was about all the kid ever hoped for when he went off to a college—more opportunities to play and prepare for coaching. On the bus to Bozeman, Erickson believed the trip he was making would probably lead to a career in coaching. That, at least, was his expectation after his father and Sweeney both encouraged him in that direction. "But come be a Bobcat first," Sweeney said, because he understood Erickson was heading to the last place he would play football.

Dennis Erickson learned how to achieve the things he

wanted in life through football while he was in Montana. Montanans always supported and appreciated his efforts as if he were an adopted son, a tough kid with some ability and desire who would find a way. He was a lot like the people who already lived there. And making Erickson's transition into football at MSU was Sweeney, tinkering with an option-oriented offense somewhat similar to the one Bill Dunn coached at Everett, which Erickson knew well already. Erickson was somewhat confident he'd have a chance to get behind the wheel at some point in his college career, and he was right.

5

Bear Bryant and the Coming of the Wishbone (Late 1960s)

The Alabama football mystique, forged out of the January 1, 1926, Rose Bowl victory over Washington, was alive and thriving in the 1960s under coach Bear Bryant while Jim Sweeney was climbing through the ranks as an aspiring coach.

Bryant's teams were tough, and Sweeney liked that. They won a lot, and he liked that, too. He heard about the Junction Boys episode when Bryant was at Texas A&M and loved it. "He was as tough as they got. I knew that generally because I knew he used to box," former Alabama director of athletics Mal Moore said of Sweeney, "but he was really dangerous because he was tough *and* smart. I remember he used to say, 'I like to fight those cowboys [roughneck amateur boxers in Montana]; all they want to do is fight and they have no idea what they're doing.' Coach Sweeney knew how to box and he'd take those guys apart."

There's a little-known story about the deep connection between Alabama and Washington State that goes way back, long before the Tide's ill-fated hire of Mike Price, the kid Dennis Erickson beat out for quarterback at Everett High School in the 1960s. It began long before Sweeney was named coach at Washington State in 1968.

Sweeney had been captivated by a speech he heard Bryant deliver at a coaching clinic and he vowed to never miss hearing the coach talk if he was within a day's drive. He stretched that time frame to the extreme once in 1961 when he drove from Montana to Los Angeles to listen to Bryant, stopping just once to sleep in a cheap hotel along the way in eastern Oregon. Bryant and Sweeney connected immediately and remained in contact on at least a weekly basis throughout the football season, comparing notes, sharing ideas, talking shop.

Moore had been a career backup quarterback for the Crimson Tide, his last two seasons finding him crowded out of a role by a kid Bryant brought in named Joe Namath. Following Moore's senior season, Alabama had no room for graduate coaching assistants. Bryant asked Sweeney for a favor, so it was Sweeney who gave Moore his first chance to be a coach.

"He loved Coach Bryant and the feeling was mutual," Moore said. "Coach Bryant would have him come down, put on the gear, and help coach after Montana State's last game against Montana each year. Coach Bryant respected Coach Sweeney's insights and opinions as much as he respected any coach in the country. I don't know of any other coach he ever allowed on the field to coach our team.

"One day Coach Bryant said I might have a job offer and he gave me the phone number," Moore said. "I had the football secretary make the call—collect—and I'll never forget when Sweeney answered the phone and I told him who I was and that I was calling from Tuscaloosa; there was a long pause and then I heard Coach Sweeney say very slowly, 'I can almost *smell* the magnolias.'"

Moore coached on Sweeney's staff in 1963, a few months after Alabama governor George Wallace stood in front of the schoolhouse doors at the university to block the admission of two black students to the segregated state school. That historic moment came in the summer, when most students were off campus, but the media that descended on Tuscaloosa wanted to interview someone else—Bear Bryant, coach of the Crimson Tide, featuring 21-1 over the two previous seasons and featured the exciting quarterback Joe Namath. Requests to interview Bryant went unfilled, which is why you can search through the history books and not find any comments from him on that historically significant day. It seems the coach and his entire staff were attending "a coaching clinic" in Montana. If by "coaching clinic" the public information office at the university meant fishing in Bozeman with Sweeney and his staff, talking football, it was an accurate statement.

"I heard that many years later," said Moore, passed away in 2013, "but to be honest with you, it was something I never spoke to Coach Bryant about. Can I positively confirm it? No. Would it surprise me in any way? Absolutely not."

At Montana State, Erickson was like a master's student who needed only practical experience when he arrived, and Sweeney was the ideal coach to give it to him. Sweeney never had time for excuses or complaints about minor inconveniences; he was a guy who realized that his limited resources demanded he find a way to maximize every punch he threw. Just like when he was in the ring against a brawler, Sweeney didn't mind being in a shootout of a football game if it meant the other guy was punching himself out. His teams didn't have a lot of shutouts, but they always had that puncher's chance. They would knock out an unsuspecting, heavily favored opponent in a minute, given an opportunity, some kind of break here or there. Sweeney was always looking, always crafting a way to land a haymaker. That was natural, it was the boxer coming out in him.

Erickson and Sweeney were a good match. In his own

way, each grasped his status in life and desperately wanted to make it into something more. The qualities Sweeney embodied — build tough players and fit them into a smart system — were similar to the ones Erickson learned from his father. Those virtues formed a foundation for a system he wanted to develop as a coach.

Sweeney said Erickson "was a coach at the age of seventeen. I always sent the plays to my quarterback, I called them myself, but when Dennis was halfway through his sophomore season, I allowed him to call his own plays. He understood down and distance theory when he got here and that's a concept a lot of quarterbacks don't get for a while because they always think they can make a play and save the day; they personalize the situation instead of seeing the big picture."

Erickson was nothing like that, always seeming to have a broader view of the current play blending into the next play. His insight astounded Sweeney. The kid arrived with a complete understanding of what coaches call gap cancellation, essentially an understanding of which defensive player is responsible for the quarterback, which is responsible for the fullback, and which one has the responsibility for the pitch man. Coaches back then would drill quarterbacks for a year to get them to understand such principles, but when he arrived, Erickson knew gap cancellation theory for every position on defense as well as all the disguises for those assignments.

Sweeney, who passed away in February 2013, talked about Dennis Erickson as a father would talk about a son. He mentioned love and prayer and he always came back to Erickson's mental makeup. "He was brilliant," Sweeney recalled, "but his brilliance was dedicated to football. Dennis was a good student, not just average, but a good student on his own. He was smart enough that he could have done anything, but the thing that separated him was that he was such an excellent *football* student; he was a valedictorian in football when he got here and that's what he wanted to do."

Sweeney had become an adherent of option football as a way to break out of the mental maze that had most coaches trying to play a power running game or a drop-back passing game that utilized screens and draws. The latter was a growing trend on the West Coast, but the scheme demanded certain elements that Sweeney was hard-pressed to recruit in the required quantities. The drop-back passing approach demanded big, mobile linemen, a big quarterback with a long-distance arm who could also make the touch passes, and also a big, bruising back and another, smaller one who was quick enough to get outside and had the hands required to catch safety-valve passes in the flats.

Sweeney needed an offense that could succeed with smaller, quicker, tougher offensive linemen who made defenses run laterally. It's what led him to option football and a veer offense that was a little more sophisticated than most. "We were running the option," Sweeney said, "but we were reverse pivoting and putting the ball in the belly of the fullback and reading the defensive end. Dennis was the best there was at that, I mean way, way ahead of anyone else I ever had at the position."

By the time he was a sophomore in 1966, Erickson was the team leader. If you were to draw up a player for his position, you probably would diagram someone two inches taller and maybe twenty pounds heavier than the 165 pounds Erickson carried. You would shave a few tenths of a second off his 40 speed and you would want a stronger arm that could bail him out of trouble with a rocket-launcher delivery system, but Erickson knew how to be successful without all those attributes. He was able to duck behind linemen when necessary to protect himself and he could lead receivers to his passes instead of having to pinpoint deliveries to an exacting spot on the field. Because he understood the offense so thoroughly, he kept himself out of trouble.

Sweeney maximized the gift he got from Pinky Erickson both on and off field by massaging the offense to match his quarterback's sophisticated understanding of the position and how it fit in the larger mosaic Sweeney was building. From the neck up, Sweeney got a finished product.

Erickson so completely understood how his actions dictated a defensive response that he was able to figure out ways to turn what defenses were trained to do against them. He knew how to make the defense read "run" and then pass. He was excellent at making teams question what they had been coached to do, a trait that would be central to his coaching style in years to come.

He could persuade a defender to commit too much to the pass by diagnosing from film study how the player positioned himself prior to the snap, something Erickson had learned ten years earlier, watching grainy football film on a bedsheet hung on his living room wall. Usually the positioning of the feet—pointing straight ahead or angled slightly toward the receiver—would be a telltale giveaway of the defender's intent. Erickson would play right into his expectations and then pull the ball in, turn up field, and run it into the heart of a misguided defense.

As a sophomore starter in 1966, Erickson caused some friction on the coaching staff by spending an inordinate amount of time with Sweeney in the film room. "I had some coaches get upset with me, seriously," Sweeney said.

Dennis and I would be going over film and putting together game plans before I met with the staff and there were a couple times I sort of waved them off when we were supposed to be meeting because Dennis and I were just getting so much done. I could talk to him like I couldn't talk to my coaches because he knew the players and he would tell me things the coaches didn't feel they could tell me. I'd come up with something and Dennis would point out [that] this guy didn't really have the lateral speed or maybe he lacked the upper body strength to block a certain guy on the team we were playing, so we'd devise something else, just for the game, that would fit what we could do better. I remember Dennis saying, "Why don't we try . . ." whatever it was, and as soon as the words came out I realized he was right, that was exactly what we should do, and it was the kind of thing one of the coaches wouldn't have mentioned to me.

Even as a freshman, when he barely got on the field, Erickson made an impression on Sam Jankovich, a former Montana high school coach who was coaching the offensive line for Sweeney. "It's funny, thinking back on it, because he didn't play much as a freshman, yet when I think of that year, he stands out," Jankovich said.

Denny didn't play much, but kids like him? You always remember those. He was, like they say, a coach on the field, very coachable and very competitive. He had that thing where he was going to figure out a way to win the game or make the play or whatever it was and you could see that in practice. I remember that very well, like it was yesterday, we all knew this was a special kid and, not to say anything against the others we had there or what Jim Sweeney was doing, but the truth is, we would have played him as a freshman, but that was before the time they were eligible. And Denny was tough, too. He'd do whatever it took to win, really, just a very, very focused kid walking through the door as a freshman.

It was 1965 and Erickson and Jankovich would only draw closer over time in ways neither of them could have foreseen. When Erickson took over the offense as a sophomore in 1966, Montana State went 8-2, including a four-game-win streak to open the season that helped erase the memory of the 1-7 finish to the end of the previous season. The fourth game was a 55–6 win at Fresno State in which the final score obscured an injury to Erickson's right wrist, the effects of which are still apparent. The specific play is lost to memory, but it came in the first half. Just another tackle, but on this one Erickson fell awkwardly, tried to brace himself as he hit the turf, and came away with his wrist throbbing in pain. He went to the sidelines holding the wrist and was scolded by Sweeney.

"Whattaya doin' that for?" Sweeney said, "You want those guys to think you're hurt?" Erickson apologized, explaining it was sore and might need to be taped. Sweeney glanced at it sideways for a second or two, said, "Hell, it looks OK, get some tape on it, you can still play, can't you?"

Erickson had the wrist on his throwing hand wrapped, the one he used to take the hard snap from center, the one he used to stuff the ball in the fullback's belly or pitch the ball to a tailback. Later they discovered a bone was broken. The injury didn't cause him to miss a game, but it left him unable to bend his wrist backward at all and also disqualified him for the draft. In his sixties, as the offensive coordinator at Utah, he still can't move that right wrist.

Erickson seldom threw a deep ball, but he managed to get by with short- to medium-range passes that helped conceal the lack of mobility in his throwing hand and wrist. He completed only sixty passes as a sophomore, but he constantly kept defenses off balance and began to gather a reputation around the Big Sky Conference. He was named All-Conference as a junior when the Bobcats went 7-3 and gained the image of being a tenacious team. The cohesive character of the 1967 Montana State team allowed the Bobcats to maintain their winning streak over rival Montana, whose coach, Jack Swarthout, had populated his staff with an assortment of the of Northwest's best coaches.

Swarthout accepted the lure of rebuilding the football program at his alma mater, Montana, in 1967. Coach Hugh Davidson, who went 8-20 after three seasons, had hired Jack Elway as an offensive assistant in 1966. It was a convenient fit for the new coach to be working with his old high school quarterback, who had followed Swarthout in the job at Grays Harbor Community College and had been nearly as successful as his mentor.

Never satisfied with doing things the way everyone else did them, Swarthout called a practice at Montana and introduced a twist in the offensive line that opened the door to more creative exploration. They flip-flopped assignments from the traditional approach that had smaller players at guard and center and the biggest lineman outside, playing the tackle positions. Teams put their biggest linemen at the two tackles for more heft against a pass rush, but Swarthout had a different idea.

"We ran that old belly series stuff out of the I formation that everybody used back then," said Bob Beers, one of twenty-four junior college players Swarthout brought in for his first season at Montana, "but Jack did it a little different. He would have the quarterback 'ride' the fullback and either give it or pull it back; he wasn't the only guy who did that but he was the first one I knew who would then pitch it to the back. This was before the wishbone; this is just how Swarthout ran the belly series out of the I—nobody else was doing that.

"Then he took the biggest linemen and put them at guard and center and he put the smaller, quicker guys outside at tackle," Beers continued. "That way they couldn't knock our big guys around in the middle and it made it easier to establish the line of scrimmage. It was really pretty innovative for the time and it was a big deal in helping us run that belly series of his."

When Swarthout left Texas to return to his alma mater, Darrell Royal continued his customary pattern and hired one of the top high school assistant coaches in the state. Emory Bellard had been coaching San Angelo Central High School with great success. He became the offensive coordinator after Swarthout, when the Longhorns were struggling and Royal's ability to lead them was being questioned. In three consecutive seasons Texas had lost four games, at least double what was considered acceptable at the school. Royal and Swarthout kept in touch. Royal implemented Swarthout's big guard concept, but he wanted more. He asked Bellard to come up with something, and one day after the 1967 season Bellard lined up some former players and showed Royal the basics of what became known as the wishbone offense.

Royal's desperation—he had turned down an opportunity to take his team to the Bluebonnet Bowl out of anger and fear of being embarrassed—was such that he put his trust in Bellard's new scheme. The next year was history.

Bellard and Royal installed the wishbone offense at Texas in 1968, though somewhat similar schemes had been used previously. Years earlier Bellard was an assistant at Alice High School, west of Corpus Christi, when Coach Ox Emerson, who had been a guard for the Detroit Lions, used something like the wishbone. Emerson wanted another blocker for his running backs so he moved a guard into a fullback-type position just behind the quarterback, giving the fullback a run at a block as the ball was snapped.

Royal and Bellard had discussed different ways to ignite the offense in 1967, when the Longhorns went 6-4 and averaged just over eighteen points a game. Gene Stallings was successfully using an option offense at Texas A&M—where he had been a member of the historic Junction Boys team coached by Bear Bryant—and when Royal watched the Aggies beat Alabama in the 1968 Cotton Bowl, he was willing to invest in something similar in Austin for the new season. It was a mixture of the option that Stallings had run with the big blocking back concept at fullback that had been bouncing around in Bellard's head for years.

At Royal's invitation, Swarthout took his entire staff to Austin for spring drills in 1968 and came back with the same blueprint for the wishbone that Royal had just implemented at Texas. "That next year," said Beers, "there were two teams in the country that ran the wishbone offense—the University of Texas and the University of Montana."

Swarthout's third and fourth years at Montana were among the best the school knew to that point. Both teams went undefeated in the regular season and reached the Camellia Bowl, essentially part of the national championship for what are now Division II and Division III schools. Swarthout lured some of the region's top coaches to join his staff, including Jack Elway from Grays Harbor Community College and Pinky Erickson from Cascade High School in Everett.

In 1968 and '69 Royal's wishbone was seen as a cutting-edge innovation at the highest level, and soon after, teams all over the country were using it. Not nearly as much attention was afforded Swarthout's wishbone, but in the smaller world of Big Sky Conference football he was properly seen as an innovator when he arrived at his alma mater as head coach. Not many reporters in those days traced his career back to Hoquiam, where Swarthout's detailed mind had started shaking up standard football orthodoxy.

Swarthout was the rawboned guy Beers saw at Montana doing one-handed pushups as the team loped out on the field for practice. Thirty years later, in his seventies, when he was an assistant for his former quarterback on Jack Elway's spring team in the NFL's European League, Swarthout could still be seen doing those one-armed pushups like a Jack LaLanne clone.

Swarthout's teams were every bit as tough as Sweeney's, and the rivalry between the schools—the Brawl of the Wild—always lived up to its name. The 1967 game, the first of two in which father and son were on opposite sides, just as they had been in high school, was won by Montana State, 14–8. Not long after that season, Sweeney announced he'd accepted the head coaching position at Washington State, replacing Bert Clark. As soon as he got there he began filling staff positions. Among the first two he hired were Pinky Erickson and Sam Jankovich, Dennis Erickson's old line coach when he was a freshman at Montana State. It was later that Sweeney hired Pinky's pal from the Montana staff, a guy with a good eye for talent and an open mind for offensive football, Jack Elway.

6

Basketball on Grass (1970s)

In the winter of 1969 Jack Neumeier felt like he needed to make something happen. It had been ten years since he began coaching at Granada Hills High School and he knew at some point the school board and the booster club guys would be asking for a bigger payoff. He didn't know when, but in the winter of 1969 he felt it coming closer.

He had done everything by the book, building a run-oriented team with a defensive mindset, playing safe, and trying to minimize mistakes at every turn, but in that year's playoff game against Long Beach Poly Neumeier's Granada Hills team lost, 7–6, while not allowing their opponents past midfield. The winning touchdown was scored on a punt return. Despite the obsession with limiting mistakes — or maybe because of it — the Highlanders fumbled three times inside the Poly 10-yard line.

The loss left a deeper scar than earlier playoff defeats. It was a more pronounced link in a chain of events that had ended badly. The most recent, gut-wrenching part of the loss was that it epitomized the futility of a string of good regular seasons followed by a playoff loss, usually to a team with much more speed. Something had to change.

Granada Hills High School is located in an upper-middle-class, predominantly white school district northwest of Los

Angeles. Throughout the 1960s the team lacked the speed to compete with teams it inevitably encountered in the post-season. The Highlanders always had some speed here and there, and Neumeier tried to use it as much as possible, but they were consistently unable to match up with the faster teams they met in the playoffs. Neumeier faced a coaching truism when he realized there is no way to properly prepare for speed. You can't practice against it, because you don't have it available, and while talking about it may have some value, at a certain point only the experience of playing against speed can adequately prepare a team to defend against it. Speed is a physical attribute that can be properly understood only through the lessons taught by personal experience.

Accordingly, Neumeier did what all good coaches were supposed to do. He increased the emphasis on defense and ratcheted up the ball-control mentality on offense. In the most accepted coaching theory of the time, those two components would work together to consume the clock and keep the ball away from faster teams. Defense and ball control would be the keys, but in that final game of 1969 against Long Beach Poly, it was turnovers by Granada Hills that decided the game.

Maybe the constant psychological drumbeat of not making mistakes had worked against them. Perhaps by focusing too much on not doing that one bad thing, they had done that one bad thing. Long before Neumeier succumbed to cancer in 2004, shortly after he attended the Pro Football Hall of Fame induction of his most famous player, John Elway, he was known for his remarkable capacity to grasp big ideas. Neumeier was like a natural-born mathematician who gets algebra intuitively when everyone else has to have it explained. He could picture how offenses and defenses operated when well executed and he had an ability to work backward from that understanding to build the drill structures that would lead to those moments. It was how he pieced together the schemes he had been using at Granada Hills for the last decade, but his grand plans couldn't account for variables such as fumbling in critical situations.

Neumeier began to read voraciously about other concepts, starting with pass-oriented derivatives of the T formation. He harbored more than a slight interest in the run-and-shoot, a passing offense that had been used successfully by Ohio high school football coach Glenn "Tiger" Ellison, who wrote a book about it. But Neumeier wasn't a run-and-shoot guy, though he did discuss it with a fellow high school coach, Darrel "Mouse" Davis, who was in Oregon at the time.

Attention to Davis's offense eventually went national in the late 1970s, when he coached at Portland State University and his quarterback was Neil Lomax, who went on to a successful NFL career. Davis eventually took his offense to professional football in the Canadian Football League, the United States Football League, and the NFL. His protégé, June Jones—another Portland State quarterback—used the offense as a coach professionally with the Atlanta Falcons and later in record-breaking seasons at Hawaii and Southern Methodist.

The swirl of media interest in Davis and his prolific quarterbacks on the West Coast obscured what Neumeier was doing in the suburbs of Los Angeles. Davis and Neumeier were creating pass-oriented offenses that worked for them, but they surely had their own specific preferences.

There has been speculation in recent years about the influence of the run-and-shoot on the first wave of spread offenses, but Neumeier made a definitive choice to go in a different direction. For instance, discussing the spread in his 2010 book *Blood, Sweat and Chalk*," Tim Layden wrote that Neumeier's first quarterback, Dana Potter, mentioned that Neumeier talked about reading a book by a high school coach in Ohio, a clear reference to Tiger Ellison's run-and-shoot primer. Much of what Neumeier read about football strategy informed his perspective on the game, but he was never a stenographer or an imitator, something Davis always knew about him. "I don't think I ever met him in person but we chatted a few times," Davis said. "He was definitely interested in the idea of the run-and-shoot—you can tell when a guy's just making conversation or he's really interested—but he was looking for something different. He wasn't fully on board with what we were doing, he wanted his own boat."

The big picture of forcing the defense to spread out fascinated Neumeier, but he was less enthusiastic about other aspects of the run-and-shoot. For one, he wasn't enamored with the slotback concept, in which two running backs or receivers were positioned outside the tackles, able to run short routes beneath defensive coverage. Neumeier thought slotbacks attracted too many defensive players too close to the ball, which clogged up the middle of the field, obligated you to throw, and denied the offense the special advantages of a tight end who can block, catch, and go in motion to confuse coverages. Neumeier wanted to throw the ball more, but he also wanted to be able to run it by dictating where linebackers had to play, so they weren't hanging around the middle of the defense. Neumeier felt the run-and-shoot limited offensive ingenuity. He was looking for an offense that could completely open up the middle of the field and send a lone running back into the wide-open space.

Also, the run-and-shoot is based on a concept of allowing receivers the ultimate freedom to run to get open. That is, receivers take any coverage the defense gives and then use it to find open space.

In the run-and-shoot the quarterback and receivers read the defense, but the quarterback essentially throws where he sees the receivers are headed. Davis used to have small receiver/running backs in the slotback positions and he would instruct them to run inside routes in front of linebacker coverage and simply drop to the turf and halt the play after receiving a pass in traffic instead of taking hits in the open field.

Neumeier grasped the general concept, but he was looking for something that would add more stress on defenses and create more opportunities for bigger plays. To say he used the run-and-shoot as a boilerplate for his offense would be like saying the I formation was copied from the T formation. True enough, the I formation grew out of what passed for the modern passing game's birth in the T formation. But they are completely separate entities, just as Tom Landry's 4-3 defense that allowed the new middle linebacker to play over the center was a defined departure over previous defensive alignments.

By his own account, Neumeier's spread offense didn't come from reading Tiger Ellison's book. It came from watching a basketball game.

The flash of inspiration came one night in the stands at a game at Granada Hills. Neumeier was sitting with his wife watching the Highlanders struggle against a bigger, more athletic team. "It was kind of like what would happen to our [football] team," Neumeier said in a 1995 interview. "You were limited by that athleticism on the other side of the ball." He was thinking about that when the light went on. It was a moment of brilliance that would eventually change not only the way football is played on the field but also the basic framework for even thinking about how to play the game.

Neumeier's insight worked against conventional coaching theories of the time, which held that you needed big, fast receivers to open the passing game. From watching a high school basketball game, Neumeier realized it wasn't just size and speed that determined whether a player could get open, it was also spacing and timing. In time, completely different body types would be required to play linebacker. The old Dick Butkus prototype could be placed in a football museum somewhere, because guys built like him would be cycled out of the game or converted into down linemen by the demands of the spread. Strong safeties would be bigger, a hybrid of a fast linebacker and a big defensive back, and pass-rushing duties would be the province of outside linebackers, lighter than the old defensive ends but much quicker. College teams would average fifty passes a game, some of their quarterbacks never taking a snap under center. Safeties would become the captains of industry on defense, controlling the game from that location as middle linebackers once did.

The spread is the key, an indispensable meaning locked into the word itself. When it was started by Neumeier and carried off to college by Jack Elway, the idea of spreading the defense was based on forcing the thick-legged linebackers to get out and move, to defend their areas from the pass, not the run.

Decades later the spread forced defensive changes and created the Cover 2 defensive system, in which agile middle linebackers backpedal into coverage at the snap; as a result, the spread generated its own answer by adding a read-option element for the right kind of quarterback. At West Virginia, Pat White would read the movement of the defensive end, pitching to a back if the end came to him, running it himself if the end went after the back, just as Jack Swarthout was teaching his offensive squad to do at Montana in the 1960s.

The worst-kept secret is that, with the right personnel, the spread always has an answer for defenses because a spread-out defense has to cover offensive players one-on-one by necessity. Whether it's four or five receivers running routes in single coverage or a running quarterback like White, Tim Tebow, or Cam Newton breaking into the second level of a defense against a defensive end, a defense that is spread apart is a more vulnerable defense.

In the winter of 1969–70, sitting in the stands at a high school basketball game, Jack Neumeier saw the future of football. Years later he remembered that the Granada Hills center was only about six foot one and posted low in the lane, arms up at shoulder height to better facilitate receiving an entry pass from the wing while being guarded from behind by a much taller defender. "I was watching this the whole time and it finally hit me," Neumeier said.

It wasn't that hard to get the ball into the post. I'm watching basketball, and my focus was on how difficult it was for the kid to do anything after he got the ball, he was completely mismatched. I was thinking, "This is like us in football, overmatched," when the whole thing made sense all of a sudden.

I thought, "Wait a minute, we don't play basketball, all we're trying to do is get a few yards." I realized if I can get a guy in front of a guy, like that center did down there, and get the ball to him in a hurry for five yards, we win that play.

Neumeier said he went home that night, got out a yellow legal pad, and began jotting down ideas. It soon got very complicated, but that was the way he worked. Nobody else had to understand it as long as he did.

"I started blocking out the field in three-yard rectangles at the line of scrimmage," he said. "Essentially, one diagonal step from here gets you here, and when the cornerback or linebacker covering you is playing to the outside, you take that step into the next quadrant inside and you're open."

At first, Neumeier had two wide receivers a step inside the sidelines on either side of the line of scrimmage, with the tight end close to a tackle on one side or the other. Then he moved the tight end halfway between a tackle and a receiver. That left a quarterback and two backs in the backfield, but if he put a back in motion, the defense had to respond by sending someone—a linebacker or safety, usually—in that direction. Now he had four eligible receivers and generally only one pass rusher to worry about. The remaining back could be assigned to block the rusher, but with a quick pass it didn't matter, the rush couldn't get there before the ball came out.

One of the significant differences from the run-and-shoot was that Neumeier's design was intended to have receivers pull coverage with them, creating more open space. In the run-and-shoot receivers wanted to frustrate pass coverage by working against what the defense wanted them to do, but in Neumeier's offense it was part of the plan to take what the defense was giving. They would, in fact, take the defense right out of the play by creating space. If a receiver was double-covered, it was an offensive victory—keep running the route, take two with you, and that will guarantee someone else is going to be wide open.

If by copying the run-and-shoot you mean doing the opposite of the run-and-shoot, then Neumeier was a copycat. He saw the future that night at a basketball game. Jack Neumeier had his offense.

It was a surprise to everyone who saw it the next season, most of all Dana Potter, Neumeier's senior quarterback. "He pulled me aside one day in the winter of 1969–70," said Potter, who would be playing his final season on a team hard-hit by graduation. "We had lost a couple of real heartbreakers in '69 and it was one of those years that was seen as our best shot to do something in the playoffs because we were so experienced. Coach said, 'We're going to go to something new next season, we'll be passing probably thirty-five or forty times a game.'"

"He might as well have said, 'We're going to all get together and flap our arms and see if we can fly,'" Potter added. "I mean, it sounded crazy to me. We're there in the San Fernando Valley, with a population over three million, and I just had this season as a junior where I passed for 998 yards; I was second by 4 yards for the most passing yards in the valley and now we're going to throw maybe three times as much, with me the only returning starter?"

Neumeier's spread offense caught fire. Potter threw for more than 3,100 yards his senior season, which he capped by leading Granada Hills to a memorable City Section 4-A championship game victory over San Fernando Valley. He went from a five-foot-eleven junior quarterback not being recruited to a quarterback signed by Nebraska. "I wouldn't have been recruited anywhere, had it not been for the spread," Potter said. "When you throw for more than 3,000 yards, it attracts attention."

Neumeier kept the system as simple as possible, with only a few passing plays that could be run in a variety of ways. He drew them up, explained them to the offense, then let Potter and his receivers work on them throughout the summer.

This is what he drew up: Two wideouts and a receiver split to one side or the other, with a man in motion who would be a fourth receiver. A single running back who could block, run, or catch a pass. A quarterback who could get rid of the ball quickly. It was designed to spread the defense thin, creating one-on-one pass routes. If the cornerbacks lay off, throw quick slants. "The quarterback takes one step back and fires," Neumeier said. "If the receiver doesn't look up, the pass is going to hit him in the head."

His inarguable logic was that if the cornerbacks played close coverage, a completed pass would gain yardage but a missed tackle could turn that 5-yard pass into a 20-yard advance. If the defense overloaded its pass coverage, they would hit the seams with the running back.

"It was a totally new concept," said Darryl Stroh, an assistant who eventually succeeded Neumeier as head coach. "He just went home and came back with this whole new flying circus thing."

In the process, Potter went from a junior disappointed that his team missed a big chance with a veteran squad to being the kid with a sweet tooth in a candy store. "They started up the first passing league in the area we ever had that summer [before the 1970 season]," Potter said. "It was sort of low key for everyone, but we had just been working on these new [passing] routes and getting the ball out quickly, so we were really fired up. We won that league and I think that gave us a little more confidence than we would have had otherwise when [fall] practice started."

Granada Hills opened the season in Las Vegas with a game against Western High School. The new approach left them behind 14–7 at halftime. "Coach Neumeier was very calm," Potter recalled. "He said we just weren't concentrating on the offense, that we had dropped too many passes and we needed to watch our reads; the whole system was based on reading the defense, and everything he said was right on the money, we all knew it as soon as he mentioned it." The Highlanders used their heads and their hands in the second half and won, 34–17. "That game gave us all the confidence we needed," Potter said. "We knew what we were doing was going to work, we just needed to keep working on it."

That first year, several teams tried to intimidate Potter by sending two or three rushers at him when the ball was snapped, but he simply got rid of it before they could get to him. The more it happened, the slower and less determined pass rushes became. "There was a lot of frustration from those teams," Potter said, "a lot of talk about it being a gimmick and all the rest. It was like the old thing about the big bully on the block who says, 'Just stand still so I can hit you.' We got a lot of that kind of thing. It was tough for the defenses because when we were running it right, anything they did as far as coverage was wrong."

By the end of the first week of fall practice, Neumeier had Potter calling all his own plays in the huddle, which is how it was supposed to work. A cycle of information kept the offense ahead of the defense throughout the game because receivers would run patterns based on the coverage they got from the defense and from picking up any weaknesses in the individual defenders.

Neumeier invested the time to give his quarterback a presnap read that would alert him to which defensive players were covering which receivers. Usually, he would break the huddle with two backs, then send one in motion to see which linebacker or safety went with the back. If it was a safety, the quarterbacks knew they could almost always drill a pass to the back before the safety could provide adequate coverage; a linebacker was usually too slow to cover the back, but if not, the motion back became a great decoy to take that linebacker out of the play.

"Then there was another read after the snap," Potter said, "where you'd look at the outside linebacker or the corner in coverage and you would adjust accordingly. If the guy was in an inside coverage, the pass would go outside; if he was out there forcing you inside, we'd take it.

"Jack Neumeier was a genius at this stuff," Potter added. "The offense wasn't as limited as the run-and-shoot, although that first year we didn't really have to get too sophisticated with it."

In time, defenses became willing to spread out to deny the pass or try to make an interception, which gave them better pass coverage, but the spread took away the middle of the field, opening the space for a running back. "Coach taught us the value of communicating, so we would have a huddle before the huddle," Potter recalled. "The receivers would tell me, 'This guy is only playing me inside,' or 'This guy is playing short, after five yards he leaves me alone,' stuff like that.

"A lot of times," Potter said, "we could just take whatever we wanted based on how they lined up against us. Every play that worked encouraged us to communicate more, pay more attention to the defense, and concentrate on our pass routes. We had film we could watch but, honestly, after about three or four games, we quit watching because it didn't matter, there was nothing to see; every team we played against after that first game had some kind of approach to playing us they hadn't used against anybody else, so it was just a waste of time to pay attention to stuff you weren't going to see."

The offense completely changed Neumeier's way of thinking about football, as he described to the *Los Angeles Times* after his retirement. "We went from designed running plays that had no chance to score to not even running a play," Neumeier said. "We were trying to score. I became a much better coach after I gave up defense. That hard-nosed stuff is not fun like offense."

Neumeier was joking about the last part, but it's true that once he came up with the spread—newspapers called it "Happy Jack's Flying Circus"—he paid less attention to defense and concentrated on scoring points. The obsession with clinging to the ball and hoping the clock runs out while you're still ahead gave way to scoring points in bunches and wanting to keep playing all day.

Potter took to the offense right away and enabled the Highlanders to immediately reach the playoff success they had missed the previous decade. He later accepted a scholarship to Nebraska and played behind Jerry Tagge and then David Humm before realizing he wouldn't get on the field for the Cornhuskers. He transferred to Iowa and eventually returned home to play in the same offense he learned in high school, just down the road at California State University–Northridge. Potter had a couple of NFL tryouts but eventually went into business and became successful in real estate.

Neumeier knew he had discovered a winning design, but not even he had any idea how good it could be until a kid named John Elway showed up in school one day. "The spread offense, as they call it now, was all I knew about football," said John Elway of his introduction to the offense at Granada Hills. "It was the first time I really played the game. Coach didn't call it 'the spread,' it was just Jack Neumeier's offense. We threw the ball quick, we used one-back sets, empty backfields; that was our offense. I think of it as the first offense I ever played in because back at Pullman I was more interested in basketball and baseball, not football."

Elway's father knew something about coaching football, and he had seen a lot of players with varying degrees of skill. Good thing his son listened to him.

"Dad had to talk me into turning out for the junior high

team in Pullman, where they were running the single wing," John said. "Of course, I wanted to be a halfback, but again, after a talk with Dad, I changed my mind. He convinced me to play quarterback.

"When we lined up at Granada Hills, it was just a lot of fun to play and I just thought everyone had an offense like ours; it didn't sink in at first that none of our opponents were playing like us."

Neumeier's offense would have been difficult enough to defend with Elway playing quarterback, but the thinking part of the game, the part that Swarthout had always emphasized to a young Jack Elway, capped it off. "Teams didn't use much motion back then and we were doing it all the time, along with throwing quick passes off it," John said. "We were so basic, so simple, and yet just our formations threw off defenses. For instance, we had one play that was off our motion. The play was that if the defense didn't send somebody with the motion guy, the play was to throw to the motion guy.

"Best of all," added the quarterback, "the play worked."

With Elway rocketing passes, the spread took flight for obvious reasons. Why it took years of success at a prominent California high school before a coach was willing to try out the spread in college is something that takes some explanation.

7

Picking on Mike Singletary
(Mid to Late 1970s)

Jim Sweeney's time as coach of the Washington State University football team was tantamount to an eight-year ride on the Wild Mouse at the state fair. He won exactly five games in the first three years with his rump-turning veer offense that featured a couple of running backs reverse pivoting away from the flow at the snap of the ball and then spinning into the direction of the play.

For Sweeney, the veer was a way to cope, to gain a little leverage against the bigger schools, where it was easier to recruit. They had trouble getting top talent from northern and southern California to even visit Pullman for a look-see, much less convincing them to commit once the recruits got an eyeful of the place located on the eastern Washington border, surrounded by rolling fields of wheat and lentils.

The veer forced defenses to hold their ground, which allowed the offense a better opportunity to block what were often more talented opposing players. The reverse pivot at the snap was just a little buffer that allowed blockers to get engaged before linebackers knew where the play would go. It was a fun offense to watch, it gave the Cougars a distinctive flair, but it didn't generate a lot of success in winning football games.

Sweeney put together a noteworthy staff of assistants over

those years from 1968 to 1975. It included Pinky Erickson from the University of Montana and Sam Jankovich, the former Montana State line coach. After a couple years Jankovich was drawn toward athletics administration and took a job for a time managing a Montana school district's athletics programs before he was hired to be Washington State's athletic director in 1972, a job he held for ten years.

Sweeney also hired Leon Burtnett and Joe Tiller in 1971, both of whom later became head coaches at Purdue. Tiller had coached for Sweeney at Montana State and later went to the Canadian Football League before returning to the states and Purdue. When Tiller went to West Lafayette in 1997 and brought the spread offense with him, he told all who would listen that it would change the way they played football in the Big 10 Conference. They laughed at him, but he was right. When Tiller retired after the 2008 season, the Big 10's awareness of the spread was practically complete, with only Iowa holding out in a more conventional, pocket-passing offense.

Mike Price, the high school quarterback Dennis Erickson beat out for the starting job as a sophomore, was hired by Sweeney in 1974 and stayed through Sweeney's eventual departure. Price lasted through the one-year stay of Jackie Sherrill in 1976 and was retained by Warren Powers in 1977. When Powers also bolted after a year, Price followed him to Missouri and used that offensive assistant's role to land his first head coaching job in 1981 at Weber State in Utah.

Sweeney hired Jack Elway off the Montana staff in 1972 to help the Washington State offense. He put him charge of recruiting the Los Angeles area, which turned out to be a determining factor in the expansion of offensive football.

After the 1975 season Sweeney took an offer from Fresno State and Elway departed for suburban Los Angeles. Elway saw film of the offense Jack Neumeier had installed at

Granada Hills High School and found it to be both a fascinating departure from anything else he had seen and a concept with great potential for college football.

It was a testament to Elway's increasing reputation on the West Coast that California State University–Northridge hired him as its head coach after he served three years as an assistant on a Washington State team that produced a 10-23 record during his time there, including just a 5-17 mark in the Pacific-10 Conference. He knew the surrounding area from his recruiting and jumped at the opportunity to move his family into the Granada Hills district. His son John had played one year of junior high football in Pullman, and wanted to be a linebacker, but Jack had seen him throw a football. He convinced his son to give the quarterback position a try after they moved.

John Elway was an incredible athlete by any view. He became a Hall of Fame quarterback, one of the best to ever play the game, but he also was selected by the New York Yankees in the 1981 Major League Baseball draft and played a season for them in the minor leagues. Basketball? Oh yeah, he knew that game, too. John Elway didn't just grow into a great athlete in high school or at Stanford University, he was born that way.

"In 1973, I was a grad assistant in the football program here," said Bill Moos, Washington State's athletic director. "It was summertime and I was up at Jack's house for a cookout or something. I'm a good-sized guy back then, six foot three, about 245, and I had played some basketball; I wasn't a bad basketball player.

"Here comes John, he's a seventh grader, okay? Jack is over there mixing a vodka martini and John's tugging at my shirt, he wants to play on the basket out back."

Moos was eyeing the martinis but went along with the kid to play some one-on-one. "I'm still in pretty good shape at that point, I ask what the game is and John says it's twenty-one, that you keep it if you make it and you have to win by two, so off we go," Moos said. "John beats me 21–3 and I felt like I barely had a chance to touch the ball, so we play again and it's 21–4. I'm sweatin' and getting a little worked up about it because I'd never lost that badly before to anyone.

"I look over and see Jack laughing at this—he'd seen it before—and I have to go one more time. John beat me 21–3 again, I look over at Jack, and I said, 'Coach, I'm too old to play basketball.'

"That's most talented athlete I'd ever been around," Moos said, "and he was a couple years too young for high school."

As it happened, John Elway's physical growth made him ready for new vistas about the time he headed to high school, and as it happened, that's when his father was looking for a job after the whole wsu staff was released following the 1975 season.

When Sweeney left Washington State he famously mentioned that he moved for health reasons. "They were sick of me," he said. At Fresno State, one of Sweeney's first orders of business was to enlist Dennis Erickson, who by then had married and started a family with Marilyn. Erickson had been 8-1 in his only year as a high school coach in Montana, and he spent time at Washington State as a grad assistant as well as a running backs coach and most recently had put in two years as Idaho's offensive coordinator. Sweeney named him offensive coordinator at Fresno State, a major step up in Erickson's career.

Jack Elway took over at California State University–Northridge, a four-year university located three miles down Zelzah Avenue from Granada Hills High School, and began implementing the spread offense he picked up from Neumeier. Outside of that straight, short line from high school to college, no other teams in the nation were using the spread offense.

When he arrived Elway raised the bar for football at Cal State–Northridge, which had been in existence for only eighteen years. He recorded three winning seasons and a 20-11 record, including a school record of eight wins in 1976. Budget demands caused the administration to eliminate football in 2001, and Elway remains the school's most successful football coach as well as an inductee in the school's hall of fame.

He was hired by San Jose State in 1979, the same year that John was the most highly recruited high school quarterback in the country and accepted a scholarship offer from Stanford University, about thirty minutes north of San Jose. At this point Jack Elway was committed to the spread offense, which he called "the one-back," a structure he believed could punch holes in defenses like a can opener.

Jack Elway was a thinker and a schemer, like the man he learned from in high school, but beyond all that, he was a football guy. "Dad loved to talk football with everyone he knew," John Elway said. "Football really was his life, it was everything to him. I could tell you a lot about my dad as a football guy — he was a personnel director with the Broncos after all those years spent coaching — and about what a great dad he was, but people should know that with us, it was always football and family, that's what we were all about.

"He was a curious guy," John remembered. "In a good conversation with another coach, he was like Columbo, he always had one more question. But the reason he liked Neumeier so much was that both of them were innovators, they were always thinking about changes in the game, which direction to go, things like that.

"At Washington State with Jim Sweeney, they coached the veer, and I know Dad was intrigued by the blocking schemes in that offense. I remember him talking about dream offenses that would combine spread formations with veer running and, today, that's sort of what our old [Broncos] offense has grown into."

In 2011, as part owner and general manager of the Denver Broncos, John Elway oversaw a team that used those precise theories about running the ball out of a spread design with quarterback Tim Tebow. It was enough to get the Broncos to the playoffs but Tebow, for all his gifts in that approach, was not a very efficient passer and Denver signed veteran Peyton Manning for the 2012 season.

When Jack Elway accepted the job at San Jose State he was committed to the spread offense, and he had an agreement from Neumeier to come up and help them install it that first spring. Elway had one person in mind to be his offensive coordinator to implement the system.

The new offense in San Jose was so far off the radar screen of major college football interest that preseason that nobody knew it existed. But as the spread was making its unnoticed debut, the 1979 football season closed the book on the most successful decade in the career of Bear Bryant, arguably the greatest coach in college football history. Followers of Notre Dame, Oklahoma, and to a lesser extent, Texas, Penn State, Michigan, and Ohio State may well argue the merits of their programs, but in Alabama and throughout the South Bryant's teams were, and remain, the gold standard for the game. The decade of the 1970s was a ten-chapter book on unparalleled achievement from coast to coast.

Bryant's Alabama teams of the 1970s were the best in the country. They won three national championships in the

1960s, but that was a different time, when segregation isolated southern teams from the rest of the nation and kept
the all-white teams playing against other segregated programs. Following the 24–9 victory over Arkansas in the
1979 season's Sugar Bowl, Alabama established its national credentials as a fully integrated program, achieving its
second consecutive national championship, a three-year record of 34-2 and a combined record of 103-16-1 from 1970
to 1979.

Following that bowl game, the Crimson Tide began to ebb
on the national scene. It didn't happen, as some historical
revisionists have suggested, after Bryant's departure following the 1982 season, which preceded his death by less than a
month. The decline began after that Sugar Bowl, when the
Tide went 27-8-1 in Bryant's last three seasons.

Just as surely as the 1979 season marked the end of Alabama's preeminent status, as though an ace had been lost from
college football's deck of cards, it also marked the starting
point for an emerging program of sweeping national prominence, a joker in the deck that had no history of legendary
coaches and no tradition of any notable significance in college football save for the rare upset here and there. While
traditional powers like Alabama were loosening their hold
on college football, something new was going on in South
Florida. The University of Miami didn't even have its own
stadium, nor much of a fan base, owing to it being a small,
private school in Coral Gables and also to the National Football League's Miami Dolphins. The Dolphins commanded
the attention in South Florida, having won Super Bowls following the 1972 and '73 seasons.

While both the Dolphins and the Hurricanes played in
the Orange Bowl, it was known more as the home of the
Dolphins, who were gracious enough to allow the college
team to play there on a handful of Saturdays. In the early

1970s, as the Dolphins' success effectively blocked the sun from shining light on the university, a faction of the school's board of regents read the handwriting on the wall and concluded they should pull the plug on football because of the expenses connected to a program that had met with very little success over the years. The university had already disconnected itself from its men's basketball team, in 1971, so athletics weren't considered sacred. There was grumbling over the basketball team, but it didn't last long, and with the Dolphins so popular, it was assumed people could adjust to life without a losing college football team playing in front of tiny crowds at the Orange Bowl.

When the regents got the numbers back from the 1974 season and saw that the school took an approximately $3.5-million financial bath that season, intercollegiate football at Miami looked to have all the staying power of a wet tissue on a windy day at the beach. Following a meeting, the board decided that, before moving away from football, they should hand oversight of the program to the only regent who had a background in college athletics. A reorganization of the athletic department ensued, with the newly created position of executive vice president of administration bestowed on board member Dr. John Green, who had previously been on the athletic board at the University of Georgia, where football was king and provided handsomely for the rest of the school's athletic programs.

Green was appalled by the conditions he saw with the Miami football program, from the lack of a weight room to substandard meeting rooms and practice and locker-room facilities. Having seen what a first-class facility looked like at Georgia, Green thought he understood why the Miami football program was so bad. How could it not be, given these conditions, which would be considered insufficient at most high schools in the country? He felt football might have a chance if it were allowed to upgrade facilities and bring in a good coaching staff, but he would be involved only if the regents let him do it his way. The regents agreed in 1976, and soon thereafter Coach Carl Selmer was fired.

Green began scouring the country for top coaches, all of whom said thanks, but no thanks, until he settled on the nomadic coaching wizard Lou Saban. A genuine coaching oddity, Saban had been with three professional teams and had worked for college programs at Northwestern, Western Illinois, and Maryland. He was a guy who could make something out of nothing in the short run, loved the challenge of turning things around, and had a wanderlust that put him up there as one of the true coaching rolling stones, always on the move.

As soon as Saban came in, things started happening. His national contacts helped bring money into the program, and his connections in the Northeast put him in touch with a kid in East Brady, Pennsylvania, who wanted to be a quarterback. Jim Kelly was being recruited hard by Penn State coach Joe Paterno to play linebacker, which opened the door for Saban. His recruiting pitch to kids in that part of the country wasn't unlike that of all Miami football coaches, who asked the kids if they liked playing in snow and ice and had they ever thought about playing in the sunshine, not far from the beach where friendly girls were sunbathing in bikinis in January?

Kelly came to Miami as Saban was headed out the door amid controversy after just two seasons. One day reporters told Saban a student had been thrown in the lake by three freshman football players and asked for his response, to which he replied, "Sounds like fun to me." They didn't tell him the part about the student being Jewish and wearing his yarmulke. Saban tried to explain his way out, but it was too late. Public sentiment had formed in a tidal wave against him and after two seasons and improving records of 3-8 and 6-5, he resigned and went to coach the football team at West Point.

A week later—within days of Jack Elway's hiring at San Jose State, where he brought in Dennis Erickson as his offensive coordinator to run the spread offense—Miami, through Green, secured the signature of the Hurricanes' next coach, Howard Schnellenberger. It was an immensely popular choice in South Florida because Schnellenberger was coming from Don Shula's staff as offensive coordinator of the Miami Dolphins. He talked a great game, with his booming, imposing voice and a big pipe he puffed that gave him a look like Captain Kangaroo with a whistle around his neck, but could he coach? Oh, yes, he could.

From the far west coast at San Jose to the southeastern tip of the mainland in South Florida, these two hires would eventually serve as markers of a shift in the fundamental direction of college football for decades to come. At the moment, nobody realized Bear Bryant's magical run was in decline at Alabama; there was certainly no national attention given to San Jose State's hiring of Elway and Miami's of Schnellenberger.

Erickson agreed to join Elway during a phone conversation and the head coach arranged for Neumeier to fly up to San Jose for spring drills to oversee the installation of the offense. It was there and then that Elway and Erickson first discussed the opportunities available to a team that could splay a defense wide open from sideline to sideline, allowing the quarterback and receivers to play catch all day. The concept was so simple, so self-explanatory, Erickson felt as though a veil was lifted that had obscured a clear vision of how to attack defenses stacked against the run.

His father had used a package of plays that spread the defense when he coached at Cascade High School almost twenty years earlier, so the general concept wasn't completely foreign to Erickson, but after playing collegiately in the veer and then coaching various offshoots of option-heavy offenses during his days as a grad assistant at Washington State and as a paid assistant at Montana State, Idaho, and Fresno State, he had almost forgotten about the possibilities inherent in the attack.

The spread offense was, in a word, revolutionary, even at a time when forward-thinking coaches were developing new ways to incorporate more passing into the strategic fabric of the game. Bill Walsh had created a short-passing offense as offensive coordinator for the Cincinnati Bengals in 1970 after strong-armed quarterback Greg Cook suffered what turned out to be a career-ending shoulder injury in 1969. Next in line for the Bengals was Virgil Carter, a player who lacked the physical gifts of Cook but possessed an exquisite mind, capable of assimilating the complicated playbook Walsh designed. Walsh came up with a system that utilized every inch of the field, from sideline to sideline, forcing coverages out of the center of the field where they could gang up on receivers.

Walsh's was a short-passing game intelligently designed to exploit defensive weaknesses with a bombardment of offensive sets and precisely drawn pass routes whose tendencies were impossible to detect prior to the snap. Walsh would have a variety of pass patterns that could be run out of a half-dozen or more offensive alignments, so the defense never had a presnap read on the play that was coming. The system—later called the West Coast Offense when it delivered five Super Bowl trophies to the San Francisco 49ers, three on Walsh's watch and two under his disciple and lieutenant George Seifert—required a great deal of time and understanding on the part of everyone involved. It also made great use of two running backs as part of the pass patterns, as both blockers and runners. Walsh's offense was intricate and heady and required certain kinds of players for certain kinds of roles. Devastatingly effective against opponents when played well, it seemed to be master's-level football.

The spread was a much simpler system to install, one that most players could grasp completely in three or four practices. In 1979 at San Jose State, the same year Walsh brought his offense to the 49ers, Elway and Erickson began to install this simpler system. With one or no backs behind San Jose quarterback Steve Clarkson, most of the passes came out after a one-step or three-step drop, which, in and of itself, rendered a pass rush impotent. Receivers were in single coverage on virtually every pass route, offensive linemen had to hold their blocks for only a second or two, and defenses soon realized they couldn't allow the middle linebacker to be wasted, standing in space a few yards behind the line of scrimmage with nothing to do. That player, considered the quarterback of the defense and the heart of its design, was suddenly useless if he couldn't effectively cover all these receivers, backs, and tight ends who would come spilling out of the spread.

Some coaches couldn't bear to take their middle linebacker off the field and paid the price, watching him struggle to play pass defense. Others took the middle linebacker out to get another safety or cornerback on the field, at which point the new offense would hand the ball to the running back, who needed just a sliver of an opening at the line to break through into an open secondary.

During Elway's time at San Jose other coaches visited to pick up whatever they could learn, among them Bob Beers, a former University of Montana player who became a high school, then college coach and later assisted Elway for three seasons in the NFL's Europe league. "I distinctly remember in 1979 one guy taking lots of notes, I mean writing down everything in spring drills," Beers said. "It was Bill Walsh." Another of Beers's memories underscores Elway's devotion to the spread even in those early days: "I remember saying one time, 'Coach, what if they get used to you because you never run the ball inside the 20, you always throw it? Maybe you should pound it in there sometimes.'

"Jack looked over with that glance of his and said, 'We don't *pound the football*. We throw the ball, that's what we do,'" Beers said. "He emphasized *pound the football* like it was a dirty word, you know? The guy was totally committed to the spread in 1979 and I know he used it before that at Northridge."

The concept took the traditional strength of a defense and leveraged it into a weakness. For decades, bigger, stronger teams had been overwhelming opponents, physically pounding them into submission. As other coaches began to use it, Neumeier's offense blew those strategies apart. At San Jose State, Erickson experienced the usual excitement and optimism that comes with a new job, but he found working with Elway and Neumeier was a transformational time in his career, the first of two big transformations that would change all he knew about football. This high school coach who had successfully implemented an original offense was the white rabbit about to take Erickson into a whole new world.

"He questioned it at first, but once we talked, he took to it immediately," Neumeier said in a 1995 interview. "After a few minutes of general discussion, Dennis saw everything. He started drawing up plays himself like he'd known it all along."

What Erickson knew was a truckload of traditional football theory; he was like a pianist who grew up with classical instruction and later wound up playing jazz that linked him to new audiences. In the knotty game of underdog football strategy, this was the one missing turn that solved the puzzle of a Rubik's Cube. Erickson and Elway spent the month of September experimenting with the offense and then won six in a row starting in October, confirming they were truly on to something.

The spread became the established offense in 1980, when San Jose State was 7-4, including a 31–26 win over Washington State in Spokane and a loss to the John Elway–led Stanford team. But it was a nonconference road game that attracted national attention and made Erickson a red-hot coaching name on the West Coast. On November 1 the Spartans went to Waco, Texas, as 29½-point underdogs to play unbeaten and No. 10–ranked Baylor. The Bears were led by future NFL draft choices, including future NFL Hall of Fame linebacker Mike Singletary, lineman Frank Ditta, running back Walter Abercrombie, and free safety Vann McElroy. Because of injuries, San Jose State started quarterback Jack Overstreet, a fourth stringer in preseason camp, against Baylor.

San Jose State's Steve Clarkson, one of the few African American quarterbacks in all of college football at the time, observed the normal game-day ritual he shared with Erickson, who would become physically ill in the hours before kickoff and liked to get out of the locker room when possible. "If it was a noon kickoff, there would be enough to do that he couldn't get out and he'd just plow through," Clarkson said. "On that day we had a little extra time because the kickoff was later so we took a walk and got some ice cream. Probably the last thing somebody would suggest, but it seemed to work for him.

"I don't remember what we talked about that day, but it wasn't about me. I was coming back from a broken collarbone and I was getting close to being ready to play again, but I really hadn't practiced at all." That changed in the second quarter when Elway told Clarkson, who had been sidelined for a month, to get ready.

"I was in complete shock," said Clarkson.

I wasn't really prepared, and I'd been looking out on the field and seeing Singletary and some of those guys hitting our people and, I mean, our guys couldn't get off the field fast enough, you know? And now they want me to go in there?

I thought Jack was crazy, because they had just kicked a field goal [for a 15–0 lead], and I was thinking, 'This is all I need,' but I gave it a go. I had noticed Singletary was manning up on our tailback [Gerald] Willhite and I thought we had some plays that might work when we put [Willhite] in motion.

We had three different routes out of that motion. One of them had the tailback kind of split the difference in his route between the x [split end] and the z [flanker], we had another that came off a vertical read where the tailback runs a kind of hitch behind [the deep-pass routes], and we had another where Singletary would have to man up on the tailback, just one-on-one. You have to remember, this was the old Southwest Conference, where it seemed like every team was running some kind of wishbone or option offense, so they didn't have their linebackers covering receivers very often and Dennis had Singletary tired by the time I got in there.

Dennis was making Singletary run all over the field. One of the things he would sometimes do would be to attack a defense by going right at the best guy, sort of [a] military tactic, like taking out the leader. I've seen him do that and other times I've seen him leave that best guy alone and go beat other guys. This time he went right after Singletary by making him run and play pass defense.

From the sidelines I could tell [Singletary] was three or

four yards behind where he should have been, he was just winded; on this particular route where he covered Willhite—because he wasn't keeping up—the slant pattern almost became a pick route, where he was going to get run into by his own guy, not because we were picking him, but because he was behind the play and the flow of it caught up with him.

"Don't get me wrong about Singletary. He had a hell of game, the guy must have had sixteen or eighteen tackles, it was just that we ran him into the ground and made him do things he hadn't practiced. Later in the game they tried to play a zone defense, but as soon as we saw that, it was like it was like taking candy from a baby.

Clarkson took San Jose State on a scoring drive five minutes before halftime that brought the Spartans to 15–7, then he hit Willhite with a 52-yard touchdown pass in the third quarter that, combined with a field goal, provided a 16–15 lead going into the fourth quarter. They added two more for a 30–22 victory that completed a trio of losses by top-ten teams that day. Previously undefeated and No. 1–ranked Alabama lost to Mississippi State 6–3, while No. 2 UCLA lost its first game to Arizona, 23–17, to go along with Baylor's loss, prompting *Sports Illustrated* to refer to it as "Black Saturday."

The other two games were classic college football upsets, but San Jose State's win was something different. "What I remember was how different it was playing against that," Mike Singletary said. "We were a Southwest Conference team in every respect; lots of tough defense, you were always playing against some kind of wishbone option, so week in and week out, you got ready for playing against a team with at least two or more likely three backs and a real physical pounding.

"Those guys came in and it was completely different," he said.

I guess it's kind of cool to think back on it as the first time people realized what the spread could do. I didn't think it was very cool at the time; it was just so weird, I don't have anything to really compare it to. We did not overlook those guys, we practiced for it, we got off to a good start, it was just so different to play against that kind of football.

When I think about it, it reminds me a little of the [1986 Chicago] Bears losing that game to the Dolphins [when Chicago was 14-0], or maybe [in 2007], when Appalachian State beat Michigan, that was the spread, too, right?

Appalachian State's victory at Michigan in 2007 got the Mountaineers on the cover of *Sports Illustrated* at the time, a more recent example of the great leveling force of the spread offense. At the end of that season Michigan hired a new coach, Rich Rodriguez, who had built West Virginia into a national power and had gained a reputation as a master of the spread offense.

By the time Rodriguez took over at Michigan, the spread had grown, branched out, and adapted an option look for quarterbacks with running ability. Coaches were discovering they could take the basic concepts of Elway and Erickson's single-coverage vision and tinker it into a spread hybrid that fit their personality hand in glove. The basic premise of making a defense give up a linebacker for a defensive back so you can run is extended one step further when there's no back and the quarterback can run it.

Back in 1980, for Elway, Erickson, Clarkson, and the Spartans, it was newer and less evolved but something they had that nobody else had. More importantly, it worked.

"San Jose State built a reputation as a passing school, a giant-killer type thing," Clarkson said, "and it all started in that game. Not taking anything away from Jack, because I loved Jack, but that was all about Dennis, at least the offense; he was like a father to us because he treated us like you wanted your father to treat you—he was explaining things, teaching, but you could always talk to him and he treated you with a respect that made you want to play for him."

After the game Baylor coach Grant Teaff voiced the sort of frustration a lot of coaches would feel against the spread. "They throw the quick stuff on offense and it's extremely tough to stop," Teaff told an Associated Press reporter. "You can't put a pass rush on because their quarterback just takes three steps and releases, so I can't really fault our defensive linemen."

What he could have done was alter his defensive alignment by removing a linebacker for a defensive back, but that would have taken Mike Singletary off the field and opened the running game for San Jose State. No coach wants to take his best players off the field, but the spread posed the ultimate question for college coaches: what if your defense is asked to do what it isn't prepared to do? It's a problem coaches are still struggling with.

Jack Elway also had a memorable quote after the game. "This," he said, "is the greatest win in my 28 years of coaching."

The Baylor upset opened the curtains of the national stage to an offense that is still gutting defenses thirty years later. Baylor's accomplished defense revealed the pitfalls that good teams would encounter if they couldn't adjust to the spread.

It was a singular moment in San Jose State football history, but for Erickson, it was just the beginning. He stayed one more year before he became Idaho's head coach. In that last season at San Jose State in 1981 the Spartans were 9-3 and finished tenth in the nation in passing and seventh in scoring. They didn't throw as often as some schools, like Brigham Young University, but San Jose was second nationally in yards per catch, with a 14.2 average.

Elway turned fifty and had become an iconic Bay Area college coach, eventually moving up the road to Stanford after John went to the NFL. His protégé, who liked to get away for an ice cream on game day, was about to do some moving, too.

8

Breaking Out (Early 1980s)

When Howard Schnellenberger took over as coach of the University of Miami Hurricanes in 1979, it had been less than a decade since major colleges in the South were all-white. He had been a coach on Bear Bryant's national championship teams in 1961, '62, and '64 all of which were all-white. It had been just nine years since the University of Southern California came to Alabama and beat Bryant's team 42–21 behind an integrated team that included running back Sam Cunningham.

That was a game said to have finally persuaded the Crimson Tide faithful it was time to recruit black athletes. Miami had been the first school in the South to integrate its football program, however, in 1967 when Ray Bellamy played for the Hurricanes. That historical note didn't register with most southern college football fans for two reasons. For one, Miami wasn't considered part of the South—anything below Tallahassee and Gainesville was too foreign in flavor—and for another, the Hurricanes were on the college football map in name only. What went on at Miami didn't matter until after Schnellenberger got involved, and then it mattered so much it took attention away from everyone else.

The University of Miami took a deep breath, decided to give football one more shot, then waited to see if the decision would prove to be sensible or negligent. The board of regents knew they wouldn't have to wonder how it turned out; they would hear about it one way or the other. What they knew for sure in Coral Gables was that they were going to make a run at seriously funding football, and that in itself would make things change.

Really, though, they had no idea what was coming.

The marriage of Schnellenberger and Miami in 1979 was about as close as it gets to heavenly matches in college football. The subtle subplot was that this former player and coach under Bryant would soon construct a team that would be the best in the decade of the 1980s, right on the heels of a fading Alabama that so dominated the 1970s.

Schnellenberger and Miami were made for each other. The school needed a megaphone and a drum major to lead a parade, and it needed someone to locate other people to be in the parade, too. Schnellenberger did it all.

Dennis Erickson, three months short of his thirty-fifth birthday when he was hired by the University of Idaho, was as deeply invested in the spread offense as any college coach in the country, although there were only three of them using it. When he got the call from Idaho, where he had previously been an offensive coordinator, Erickson, his former high school teammate Mike Price—by then the coach at Weber State College—and Jack Elway were the only coaches in the country using the one-back offense, which soon became known as the spread. Erickson had been involved for three years with the system, Price had used it for the better part of two seasons, and Elway, the first to use the offense in college football, would eventually record sixteen years of coaching the offense.

When Erickson accepted his first head coaching job for

the Division I-AA Idaho Vandals, it was on the coattails of what he had helped Elway accomplish at San Jose State. By then Erickson was fully immersed in the spread, since he had been the play caller at San Jose State and had personally orchestrated many of the Spartans' upsets. Erickson took the Idaho job in December 1981 and coached the spread exclusively for the balance of his career.

Erickson became the face of the spread offense for a couple of reasons apart from the on-field successes his teams found on a consistent basis. For one, he learned from Elway and Neumeier, the offense's most high-profile coach in the beginning and the guy who invented the damn thing. Erickson learned the offense from the creator that first spring in 1979 in San Jose and implemented it for the first time at the Division I-A level in college football in the regular season a few months later.

When he started in Moscow, coaches on the West Coast were already talking about the concept and about him. While Elway introduced Erickson to the spread through Neumeier, everybody in the business knew Jack Elway. Erickson was the new name, the one who pulled the levers and twirled the dials on the offense at San Jose State.

"When he left to go to Idaho, it was very, very difficult for all of us," said Steve Clarkson, the Spartans' quarterback. "We knew he had to go, we all supported it, but man, it just wasn't the same without him. All he ever asked was that we be prepared—that was our responsibility—and that we play hard. He got us to believe in being responsible for ourselves and trusting each other and then letting it all go on game day. I mean, how can you not play for a guy like that? We all loved him."

Erickson's personal coaching style came directly from his father, the man he watched walk the sidelines at Ferndale High games in a November downpour, the guy he saw in the float at the Labor Day parade, the guy who broke down film on the living room wall.

Now he had his own team. It felt natural.

"He stressed individual responsibility and we all went after it, we really dug into preparation, and then on Friday—this might have been unique in the whole country—we'd get the day off," Clarkson recalled of Erickson's last year at San Jose State in 1981. "His idea was, the preparation is in, we know what we need to do, now take a step back, see the big picture, and relax yourself for the game because you're going to need every ounce of energy on Saturday. Friday was like a day for being at peace mentally, just focusing, and not being out doing stupid stuff, that crap didn't fly with Dennis."

In time the media would portray Erickson as a coach who ran a loose ship, didn't enforce discipline, and looked the other way when he heard there might be trouble on the team. Clarkson never knew that Erickson and neither did his parents, sisters, friends, and colleagues who coached with him.

Clarkson took Erickson's father-figure business seriously after he got to know Erickson's parents, his wife, Marilyn, and his sisters, who talked to Clarkson about their Catholic faith. Clarkson wound up getting baptized and then asked Erickson to be his godfather. More than thirty years later, they're still close. Erickson once tried to get Clarkson to come to Washington State and be on his coaching staff, but Clarkson wasn't thrilled with the idea of living in Pullman. He started a quarterback clinic, was asked to speak around the West Coast, and eventually formed a company, Air 7, that has become one of the most successful and well-known private quarterback schools.

"I hated to lose him," Clarkson said, "and I hated it even more when he wasn't there. But even then, as a college kid, there was this feeling that this was his calling and he needed to go."

Until he was hired by Miami, Schnellenberger always thought his relationship with Bear Bryant was his most valuable calling card. It no doubt carried some weight among the board of regents in the hiring process. He soon discovered the locals didn't care about that distant college stuff, however; this was a Dolphins' town and they were more impressed that Schnellenberger had been one of Don Shula's assistants with Miami's '72 Super Bowl perfecto champions.

That was fine with Schnellenberger, who saw himself as big-time coach who needed only the right team to drive to a championship. He knew how the game was played; he'd studied it while playing for and working with Bryant. The skill set Schnellenberger brought to the job also included a small slice of a carnival barker, just the right touch for the task. With his authoritative speaking style he could have done voiceovers for Foghorn Leghorn, and Schnellenberger knew how to spin a yarn. He was a master at measuring out appropriate dollops of fact, opinion, and leaps of logic that kept reporters and television camera crews coming back for more. He was exactly what the University of Miami football program needed at that time and he was perfectly positioned to deliver.

Schnellenberger built the Hurricanes into a physically intimidating team by working them into the ground and demanding they get back up again. His practices were brutal at a time when there were no restrictions on the amount of time players could be worked each week. Having played for Bryant, generally considered to be the most demanding coach in the business, Schnellenberger built on his former coach's system and tried to take it a step further.

The most important thing he did may have been in the area of recruiting, where Schnellenberger was a rank amateur but he knew something about protecting your own turf. That was one of the problems at Miami, he figured; it didn't have recruiting turf to protect. The program had always had pretty good results selling kids from the Northeast on the joys of playing football all winter in sunny South Florida, but in chasing those recruits, the program historically had neglected its own backyard. With an assist from Saban, Schnellenberger changed all that.

Saban was the first to seize on mining the rich recruiting fields of South Florida. In the same winter of 1978 when he recruited Kelly during a snowstorm in Pennsylvania, Saban began to bring in players from the greater Miami area. A total of nineteen of his thirty recruits that year lived within an hour or two of campus.

The myth is that Schnellenberger expanded and exploited Saban's local awareness, dividing the state horizontally at about the Lake Apopka–Orlando vicinity, renaming everything south of that imaginary line as the "State of Miami" for his recruiting purposes, a public relations jackpot. Actually, it happened just the opposite of that, with Schnellenberger's assistants scouting the immediate South Florida area and counties connecting to Dade and Broward, then moving westward. Finding those areas to be just as productive, and they kept expanding out and up until Schnellenberger eventually decided to draw a line of sorts. It became the new sacred recruiting grounds, if by sacred we mean a catchy concept that brags to recruits through images of territory and turf. Screw Florida State's assumed in-state advantage, these guys were changing the subject to themselves and it was an immediate hit with the kids they went after.

This thing hit like four bars across on a Vegas slot machine. It was a quick-strike fix to a generational problem at

Miami with the soon-to-be realized bonus that it was also the long-term answer to profit-making football at the small private school in Coral Gables. Saban and Schnellenberger were swimming in the deep end of this fully stocked talent pool that served the same purpose in recruiting that an endless vein of gold would bestow on a lucky miner. In each case, their wish lists were fulfilled well beyond their own lifetimes.

And it had been there all along, just waiting. "I can't tell you why the area wasn't more strenuously recruited before we got there," Schnellenberger said in a 2006 interview when he was head coach at Florida Atlantic University, "but it quickly became our priority. There was a tremendous amount of talent and [an] unbelievable amount of speed — that's the thing [that] makes you a good coach, athleticism with exceptional speed."

Green had secured Schnellenberger's signature on a contract after agreeing to essentially turn the athletic department over to him by allowing the new football coach to pick his athletic director. That was a common practice in the South during the time Green was at Georgia and was only beginning to change around the time Schnellenberger was named head coach.

Schnellenberger selected Charlie Thornton, an assistant AD at Alabama familiar with the Bear Bryant approach to winning, but after less than three months Thornton resigned when his wife was diagnosed with cancer. Harry Mallios, a one-time Miami football player who had been teaching at the school, took over as athletic director. Mallios had the title but it was Schnellenberger's department.

Schnellenberger had barely accepted his job before he told his staff the goal was to win a national championship in five years. "I didn't have the luxury of time," Schnellenberger said. "They were talking about I-AA football and I wasn't interested in going in that direction, so we had to head in the other direction, fast."

Few have come further faster than the Miami Hurricanes under Howard Schnellenberger, but as quickly as he got the Hurricanes their first national championship, he began to feel disenchantment settle in. After his first season, one that included a rousing upset victory at Penn State directed by Kelly, who started his first collegiate game that day, Schnellenberger was informed of new budgetary constraints that would impinge on recruiting expenses and travel costs. But this would not be a meaningful setback.

Schnellenberger developed the State of Miami concept and announced the football program was headed on "a collision course with the national championship." It would be these regional kids who would win it, coming to a place where it had never been done. Schnellenberger would dive into their eyes with that piercing look of his and say, "We will bring a national championship here. Do you want to be part of that?" They built the desire for the hope and expectation of one day being a 'Cane and shocking the world.

The influx of talent from the State of Miami built a personal and regional bond of identity among the players. This self-assured taskmaster, pushing, challenging, and daring them on a daily basis, was driving them.

There was the time in 1982 when they were 5-2 going into the homecoming game against Florida State and lost, 24–7, prompting Schnellenberger to have a full-pads scrimmage the following Sunday morning. He brought with him from the Dolphins the practice of twelve-minute runs in which everyone had to meet a certain standard or do it again the next morning.

He built a winner in his second year, coaching the team to a 9-3 record and a Peach Bowl victory over Virginia Tech. By the time the school named Edward Thaddeus "Thad"

Foote II its president in 1981, when the 'Canes went 9-2 and closed out with a big win over Notre Dame, Schnellenberger was rewriting the college football map with Miami in a position of prominence.

Dennis Erickson's preparation and background were unquestioned in his new head-coaching job. He was fourteen years removed from his last game as a player and he'd worked with some of the most creative, if not the most well-known, coaches in college football. In 1982 he began coaching a program that had been 3-8 the previous year. Erickson's first season produced a 9-4 record and in just four seasons he managed to win more games than any coach in school history.

The news conference announcing his hiring came on the morning of Friday, December 11, 1981. Later that night Muhammad Ali climbed into the ring in the Bahamas for the last time, losing his final bout to a largely unknown Trevor Berbick, who five years later would be remembered as the guy Mike Tyson beat to become heavyweight champion. Berbick represented a bridge in boxing history, connecting the last act of the elegant and elegiac career of Ali to the first title in Tyson's merciless and ultimately pitiful career.

Erickson was building a bridge of a different sort in college football. He was constructing a pathway over and around the obstacles represented by the major recruiting investments required to effectively run the power offenses of the day. Before other coaches took the time to give the spread an honest, critical look, Erickson realized the potential it possessed.

The spread would be an offense for everyone because it created one-on-one matchups that allowed your best players to make plays, but Erickson discerned the difference the one-back approach could make for underdogs. If you could get a smart, aggressive quarterback with a decent arm and a few receivers, preferably with speed, you had a chance to compete.

Once players saw the offense, Erickson knew it would be a recruiting magnet for quarterbacks, receivers, and running backs. From the start, it was dismissed as a short-passing, chuck-and-duck style, but Erickson never saw it that way. From Pinky, he knew the value of being able to run and throw, and he saw tantalizing creases in the offensive line once the defense was stretched to the sidelines. He wanted to make linebackers run laterally to the sidelines to cover receivers—that was a basic formulation of the offense—but he never forgot about the running lanes that were exposed when he could get someone like Mike Singletary off his spot and in motion.

Erickson was at the figurative mesa overlooking the last frontier of offensive strategy, and he seemed to know it. His approach, for all the talk of nothing new ever happening in football, was actually quite new and separate from what had previously been attempted in the game. In a small office in Moscow, Idaho, with a coaching staff of youthful nobodies, he unhooked an offense that sent coaches from the Canadian border to Mexico running to film rooms to see what it looked like.

The Idaho staff was largely unknown nationally but well known to Erickson, which was all that mattered to him. Each one was part of a coaching fraternity that circled back in one way or another through his father, Jack Elway, or Jack Swarthout. They approached the game with such a noticeable outward confidence and swagger, you'd think they had a secret weapon on their side. Not far off the point, actually. With the exception of his father, whom Erickson named tight ends coach at Idaho, only a couple had held a full-time job on a major college staff; some had only a little college coaching experience and a few were starting their first job. What they shared was commitment and energy.

In time, three of Erickson's assistants from his first staff would become Division I-A coaches. They generated a collective force of will, ambition, and momentum matched by few staffs in the West because they had something nobody else had, and they knew it.

"Everybody was talking about it," said Keith Gilbertson, Erickson's offensive coordinator. "In the college football coaches' network back then, everybody wanted to know more about it, some guys said it was all gimmicks, but the more you learned about it, the more you wanted to know. None of us were making any money, but we were hot, we were riding a commodity that worked and we damn well knew it."

For years in the 1980s, the spread offense Erickson coached was *the* topic of conversation among the coaching fraternity in the West. When he started at Idaho it wasn't commonly known as the spread or the one-back, because it was his approach to not be a promoter of the offense in the media. He would go to clinics and talk all day with coaches, but Erickson wasn't big on positioning himself in the media as some leader of a movement.

At any one time in a game you might see just one running back behind the quarterback and you might see that player go in motion and leave the quarterback alone. It was called an "empty" backfield and when it was first seen you could hear breathless gasps in press boxes at the sight of this new invention. "Look at that," some writer in the press box would exclaim, watching a quarterback call signals with no one behind him while players scrambled wildly on defense, uncertain of their coverage assignments. "He's telling the defense he's going to pass, why would he do that?"

Actually, it was more involved than that. When Erickson's

backfield went empty, what it was really doing was dictating to the defense what its assignments would be. Heavy-legged linebackers were now forced to cover quick receivers and sometimes, by doing so, they would leave a gaping hole "underneath"—five yards or so past the line of scrimmage, where linebackers usually roam—for a running back who had been in motion to enter and receive a pass.

Erickson's diabolical instinct was to turn everything defensive players had been taught against them. If they chose to hold their position, they would have no one to block, no one to tackle, nothing to do; if they were forced into pass coverage, they were suddenly doing something they hadn't practiced during the week and their pass-coverage responsibilities took them to areas of the field where they would never stray in the general course of a game.

For an underdog like Idaho, this was the ultimate get-even weapon. When they broke the huddle, you never knew what the Vandals might do—empties, trips, opens, and bootlegs were all formations or plays that might be called on any down.

Erickson loved to play against teams with physical, aggressive linebackers who were used to blitzing quarterbacks and stuffing runs. He'd play those poor kids like a yo-yo all afternoon.

One of his first quarterbacks at Idaho was Scott Linehan, who later went into coaching and climbed through the ranks to become the head coach of the St. Louis Rams. "It was so new then that we were playing teams that had literally never seen the offense," Linehan said.

> As a coach, it's amazing to remember how Dennis approached it back then to set up the defense. We would usually come out in a regular, two-back set—teams very seldom had much motion in their offense then—and he would send one of the backs in motion to see what the defense did.

Defenses just didn't know enough about it to fully prepare, so they would usually have one guy responsible for the
motion guy; as a quarterback, when that guy would go in
motion, you could almost sense a panic in the defense; they
didn't know what was coming.

On our first series, Dennis would use different motions
to see who was covering who. Then the whole rest of the
game, he would just decide who he wanted to throw to, on
what part of the field, against which defensive back, and he
would simply motion a back the other way to clear out that
spot on the field for a one-on-one route.

It was like a chessboard to him, only he was the one who
got to move your pieces where he wanted them before he
made his move. Honestly? As a quarterback, it was an awe-
some thing to be a part of; controlling the defense like that
gave you ultimate confidence, it was almost like cheating for
the way you could manipulate the other team.

Erickson's staff was there for two reasons. One, they knew
him through some personal relationship and two, they were
frothy with desire to be a part of this new offense. Nobody
knew who these assistant coaches were, but their careers
were springboarded to attention because of the coaching
buzz that came out of Idaho in the early 1980s.

Offensive coordinator Keith Gilbertson was a childhood
friend of Erickson's from Everett, Washington; his father
had supervised Everett Memorial Stadium over the summer
when Dennis, Keith, and other kids played in loosely organized leagues. Gilbertson had been the young offensive coordinator at Utah State, then at Fresno State when they com-
peted with San Jose State for the Big West Conference title
in 1979–81, where he first got an eyeful of the spread. Gilbertson followed Erickson as head coach at Idaho and was
later the head coach at California and Washington.

John L. Smith, an Idaho native who coached at the University of Montana and was known to Pinky Erickson through his labyrinth of coaching connections, had been employed as the defensive coordinator at Weber State in Utah for Coach Mike Price before being hired by Erickson in the same role. He always used to be just John Smith, but when there are two John Smiths in the same athletic department, somebody has to blink and change the name. John L. Smith was with Erickson for six years and eventually followed him and Gilbertson as head coach at Idaho from 1989 to 1994. From there Smith went to head-coaching jobs at Utah State, Louisville, Michigan State, and Arkansas.

Chris Tormey was given his first full-time coaching job as a defensive line coach for Erickson in 1982. When he was the backfield coach at Montana State Erickson had recruited Tormey, who ultimately decided to attend Idaho. Erickson liked Tormey's aggressive approach as a player, and after Tormey served as a graduate assistant at Washington on Coach Don James's 1981 Rose Bowl team, Erickson gave him a job. Tormey later took the Idaho coaching job after Gilbertson and Smith and after that was the head coach at Nevada.

Tim Lappano had been a hard-running tailback for Idaho; Erickson recruited him out of high school in Spokane. He gained over 2,000 yards rushing in four varsity seasons, but his senior year was cut short by a torn hamstring that left him a sideline spectator. Lappano had been released from a free-agent tryout by the Houston Oilers, was out of work, and had no idea what he wanted to do with his life when Erickson offered him the job of running backs coach.

"He pulled me out of a bar," Lappano said. "I had no plans to coach, I didn't know what I was going to do with my life, not a clue." Lappano was assisting the football team at Spokane's Ferris High School when Erickson found him. He wasn't in a bar, but the metaphor for an out-of-work football junkie makes the point. He was considering employment options when Erickson gave him a job.

"When he recruited me he promised my parents I'd get a diploma and I was still twenty-some credits short, so he told me he needed to make good on that promise," Lappano said of Erickson's sales pitch. "I was ready. It wasn't what I had thought about—I really didn't know what I was going to do—but I was definitely ready to jump back in and give it a try."

Gregg Smith, retained on the staff as a graduate assistant, later became a full-time coach and was Pancho to Erickson's Cisco. Smith was the offensive line coach everywhere Erickson coached from the day Erickson took the Idaho job in 1981.

Dan Cozzetto was another Spokane kid Erickson had recruited in his first tour of duty at Idaho. "I'll never forget the recruitment," Cozzetto said. "I was out of high school, doing nothing with my life, then I enrolled at Spokane Falls Community College. I was going to try to play there when I came home one day and found Dennis sitting at the kitchen table with my mom and dad.

"They each had a Rainier beer, and my dad says, 'Come meet your new coach,'" Cozzetto recalled. "[Erickson] promised my parents I'd get a degree and the next thing I knew, I was going to Idaho." Cozzetto was on Erickson staffs at Idaho twice, at Oregon State, with the San Francisco 49ers, and at Arizona State.

It was a remarkably youthful staff, with the exception of Pinky, Erickson's father, the staff's official Yoda figure. Besides that, it was a staff that knew exactly what they were getting into and each one was prepared to make a full commitment. They were about to change the way football was played and they radiated a confidence about their mission. They all felt like revolutionaries. Well, maybe not Pinky, but they needed his old-school approach to keep the ship steady.

9

Turning Point (Late 1980s)

Mission accomplished.

In 1983, the fifth year under Howard Schnellenberger, the third year for university president Edward Foote II, Miami won the national championship, beating heavily favored and unbeaten Nebraska, a squad more closely approximating Your Daddy's Team, 31–30. It was a definitive representation of the game of the decade in the sense that it put Miami on a national stage as a football power while also foreshadowing what was to come in college football over the next decade.

Carried away by being on top of the world, Schnellenberger acted thoughtlessly and resigned in a huff, feeling his role in the department was being diminished. Foote, seen by Schnellenberger as a professional antagonist to his efforts, prompted the coach to listen to one of the most ill-conceived job offers in major college football history. Schnellenberger agreed to be the coach of a Miami franchise in a new springtime professional league—the United States Football League. The deal collapsed before it ever began when the owner took the team to New York instead of South Florida, leaving Schnellenberger without a team, without a financial commitment, and without the reigning national champions.

What played a role in Schnellenberger's eventual departure

was the hiring of a new athletic director, Sam Jankovich, earlier in the year. Jankovich was hired away from Washington State, of all places, to run a program competing for national championships in football. At that point, the only time you ever heard about Washington State athletics, it was either the school's successful baseball team or the track team. But Jankovich impressed Foote and the board of regents for reasons that had nothing to do with track and baseball and everything to do with football, a sport at which Washington State was only occasionally competitive. Jankovich was well known to both university presidents and administrators because he conceived and wrote the first buyout contract in college athletics. After Jackie Sherrill replaced Jim Sweeney at WSU in 1976, the new coach stayed one year before taking a job at Pittsburgh. Warren Powers was hired and a year later he left for a better offer at Missouri; Jankovich then created a buyout clause that said if a coach left before the term of his contract was up, he would have to pay the school what was a princely sum at the time, $50,000.

The buyout clause was soon put in virtually every contract in the country. More significant than the financial implications, it sent the message to administrators that Jankovich understood where the authority properly rested in university athletics. It wasn't in the office of the athletic director, who was often little more than a hand puppet for the football coach. As the Hurricanes gained national prominence, the Orange Bowl went from mostly empty on home game Saturdays to sold out, and network television called to put Miami on more and more often, Foote and the regents realized they wanted control of the program that just a few years earlier was being prepared for an early burial.

Schnellenberger's decision to resign was, in hindsight, perhaps the worst decision ever made by a prominent college football coach. Not only did the new league to which he fled not field the team he signed up for, the Hurricanes got better and better without him. Had he not left, Schnellenberger might well have still been coaching there, rivaling the number of national championships won by his mentor Bear Bryant.

Schnellenberger made the mistake of not getting to know the new athletic director, a former offensive line coach who wanted a national championship as much as the coach. Instead, Schnellenberger saw Jankovich as a threat to his future. He wasn't; he was only a threat to Schnellenberger's unrestricted power within the department.

It wasn't Jankovich who had removed Schnellenberger's power, it was Foote. Jankovich asked for total control of the department when Miami contacted him about the job; Foote agreed. "I wasn't going to go there and have the football coach run the athletics program," Jankovich said. "They had a football program and a baseball program and not a lot more that they did in a big way. Howard didn't pay much attention to the ground rules or anything else, so we had a heart-to-heart when I got there, but I had a heart-to-heart with [Foote] before I got there, or I never would have taken the job."

The request was simple. Jankovich would be willing to move from the Northwest to South Florida and begin the work of rebuilding the athletic department, but only on the condition that he had complete control over everyone and everything within the department. What was the worst that could happen for asking?

It sounded perfectly appropriate to Foote. It also sounded like a diminishment of Schnellenberger's authority, and it was, but Jankovich has maintained he wouldn't have been an impediment to the coach. "I didn't want to go there and try to change the way everything worked after I got there," Jankovich said. "It had to be changed before I got there or

I would not have taken the job. You can't have a situation where people are fighting over control, that has to be understood up front at the beginning."

It was understood, and there was no question about who was running the department when Schnellenberger left in June 1984, eleven months after Jankovich came aboard. Jankovich represented a controlling presence in the transformation of the Miami football program.

What Lou Saban did with recruiting home-grown Florida players in 1978 hasn't changed much since. The only difference has been in the level of competition for South Florida players. In-state schools like Florida International, South Florida, and Florida Atlantic started football programs because of the depth of available talent in the pool and others, like Central Florida and the two other main rivals at Florida and Florida State, have all benefitted from players living in the State of Miami.

What they got in that first decade or so were players from areas that felt neglected, at best, or ostracized, at worst. Many came from poor or lower-middle-class homes and often brought issues related to one-parent family life or an adolescence spent in crime-infested neighborhoods. They often came with hardened attitudes that didn't fit neatly into the environment of a private university that took pride in academics and didn't concern itself much with athletics:

The players soon became aware that the football program was being built around them and that they represented a new national power, an insurrection of sorts on the Nebraskas, Penn States, Oklahomas, and all the others who represented the ruling class of big-time college football. Once they realized the possibilities under Schnellenberger, the 'Canes wanted to make history and leave a lasting mark.

They were retelling college football's story and rewriting its history, in their image. The Miami football program was built on the talents of players from the "the other Miami," not to be confused with the trendy shops and late-night bars around South Beach. These weren't kids who grew up in the art deco condominiums of Collins Avenue, where stretch limousines transported cosmopolitan elites from shopping forays to dinner on the town at the St. Moritz and Royal Palm Hotels.

These kids were more often found in tough, low-income neighborhoods the Chamber of Commerce didn't talk about. They were athletes without the trappings of middle-class white American suburbs, where children played in well-organized youth leagues with good equipment, sponsors, and coaches who took you to Dairy Queen after games on Saturday afternoons. More often than not, the kids who built Miami football into a late twentieth-century power grew up in chaotic environments overlooked by the social and educational mainstream. Now they were being sought after like rare gems.

They got it, immediately. Nobody had to draw a picture for Alonzo Highsmith, Bennie Blades, or Michael Irvin. They understood they were suddenly objects of desire because the University of Miami wanted to use them to win football games. An unspoken mutual understanding was formed. The school was happy to bend away from its practice of recruiting in Pennsylvania and other faraway locations to bring in these players as a means to facilitate a goal; the players were just as interested in using the school as a springboard to professional football, where they could make money they saw as unavailable to them anywhere else. It was "you help me, I help you," but these new-breed Hurricanes were going to do it their way, representing where they came from, not what someone else wanted them to be.

They were comfortable in chaos; it was all many of them had known in their young lives and they would bring that clash and rattle to Miami, where they would define their own style. This wasn't going to be a squeaky-clean, white brand of NCAA football, it was going to be something all their own, a true-life depiction of the world they knew at the intersection of Controversy Avenue and Excellence Boulevard. It was going to be loud and everlasting and it would be filled with winning.

Saban, in that first recruiting class, and then Schnellenberger offered a stage for these new players and their communities as well as a national platform for the new culture they were building at Miami. All of it was completely unacceptable to the NCAA, the cartel that operates the multibillion-dollar business of college football and dictates how the game will be played as well as how it will look and feel to potential sponsors.

Miami players acted on the field the way they had learned to act in the culture they came from. They were up front, in your face; they expected to beat you and were happy to tell you as much before, during, and after the game. They strutted, trash talked, and danced their way to the top of college football's heap with a style all their own. What really stood out, though, from the first moment you saw it, was the tenacity these new Hurricanes brought to the program. They drove, prodded, and challenged each other every day in practice in ways that coaches couldn't teach; it was something they brought from home to this ragged, boisterous community they were building at the university. It was all-out, demanding, demonstrative football from minute to minute in every practice leading up to a game.

Into this combustible stew came Jankovich in July 1983, a little over a month before the start of Schnellenberger's fifth season at the school, the last year in the coach's five-year plan to win a national championship. Jankovich was startled to the point of being scared by what he saw. He'd seen a lot and knew what tough football teams were all about—they had only two kinds in Montana, the tough ones and the ones a little tougher than the others. But Jankovich had never seen anything like the first fall practices at Miami in 1983.

"I was astonished at how brutal they were," Jankovich said. "How in the world they could make those guys practice in the heat and the humidity like they did and how they all stuck with it was incredible to me.

"I looked at it and I said, 'My good lord, we're going to lose one or two of these players here,'" he said. "But you never heard them bellyache; those kids worked hard and those coaches coached hard. It took me a while to realize those kids came with that kind of raging intensity. It was a different world from anything I had ever seen."

Outside of Schnellenberger's coaching office, few took his goal seriously. The Hurricanes weren't ranked in the 1983 preseason top twenty, and they opened with a shuddering 28–3 loss to Charley Pell's Florida Gators in Gainesville. The No. 1–ranked team all season was Nebraska, with its powerful, downhill, power-I formation offense led by running back Mike Rozier, receiver Irving Fryar, and quarterback Turner Gill. The Cornhuskers benefited from opening the season in the Kickoff Classic against the previous year's national champion, Penn State. The 44–6 victory over the Nittany Lions just across the river from the world's media center in New York City put every critical eye on Nebraska, and the closer people looked, the more impressed they became.

The Cornhuskers scored fifty-six points against Wyoming in their second game and then went on the road and rung up eighty-four at Minnesota. They were a unanimous No. 1 selection, while Miami earned a bid to play them on their home field in the fiftieth renewal of the Orange Bowl as the No. 5 team after running off ten straight victories. Undefeated and No. 2 Texas was knocked off by Georgia earlier in the day and Schnellenberger arranged for an old Alabama player to say a few words to his team before kickoff. Joe Namath, the iconic hero of Super Bowl III, told the Hurricanes greatness was within their grasp that night, not failing to mention that he had led the New York Jets over the Baltimore Colts on the same field fourteen years earlier.

Miami ran off to a 17–0 lead, then won 31–30 when a late two-point conversion attempt by the Cornhuskers failed. Just as he predicted, Schnellenberger had won a national championship in five years at a place that had no reason to think, based on history, that such a thing could actually happen.

History was moving, fast. In a few weeks Bryant would be dead and five months later Schnellenberger, feeling disrespected after winning a national championship only to have his power diminished within the university, resigned. Ten months after Jankovich flew in from Pullman, Washington, to take the job, Miami was at the peak of college football's summit and he was in complete control of the athletic department. His task, simplified, was to find a coach who could win some more championships.

At one end of the country, deep down in South Florida, a new director of athletics needed to maintain a winning edge at the newest national power, while up in the far inland Northwest Dennis Erickson was tearing the top off defenses with a design he felt would revolutionize football, given the right setting.

By the time he took the head coaching job at Idaho, Erickson knew what he had with his spread offense. His coaching staff bought into it wholeheartedly and they all believed what they had would take them out of Moscow, Idaho, one day. It was never mentioned, but the idea of what that particular group of talented, homegrown, and title-seeking players on the rise in Miami, looking to overturn the orthodoxy of the NCAA, might be capable of with Erickson's offense would have been frightening.

"Dennis brought an offense that said 'Fuck you' to all those ideas about how and when to run the ball," Keith Gilbertson said.

I mean, it was as simple as that, it was the idea of doing something completely different, something none of these other coaches would ever consider because of all the unspoken rules of football coaching. Not with Dennis; we were calling bullshit on all that stuff. With Dennis, the thing was, "Let's just go score some points and then smack them in the mouth on defense with a gang-tackling attitude."

You know, some of the things he'd do to a defense almost seem cruel. Bill Walsh was passing the ball, BYU was passing the ball, and they were sort of breaking up that old run-first formula, but what Dennis was doing was different from those guys, it was edgier, more aggressive, more out there. Back in those days, Dennis would mess with your mind, he understood you so well from tape, he'd do something that would blow your mind defensively, just undress your philosophy and leave you standing there with your pants down.

He wouldn't run up the score on you, but he'd get in your head and kick your ass with theory, make you question what you teach, that kind of thing; what he did to teams back then was deep shit that left a mark on you.

It didn't hurt that Erickson knew what he needed to make the offense work and knew how to recruit. He was at Los Angeles Valley College looking at film of a prospect one day

when five-foot-nine, 140-pound receiver Eric Yarber happened to come into the room. Yarber was being recruited by
Colorado, Illinois, and Purdue. The coaching staff at Colorado knew their receiver Anthony Carter had been a favorite of Yarber's and the Buffs thought they had the inside
track on him. When Yarber came into the film room, he saw
a guy with a full head of bushy hair watching a game tape.

"He was young looking, you know?" Yarber said. "I
thought he was a friend of one of the coaches or something."
Erickson liked Yarber's informality. He thought of it as self-
confidence and preferred it to the yes sir, no sir comments
some young football players are taught to use when speaking to adults. Yarber reminded Erickson, just a little bit, of
himself.

Erickson knew who was recruiting Yarber and told him
they were probably saying that if he went to one of those
other schools, they'd be on television, they would play at
the highest level, and in time, he'd get his chance. It was as
though Erickson had been reading the scripts from other
recruiters.

"He told me if that's what I wanted, the big show, promis-
es that games would be on TV all the time, then he couldn't
compete with that, he'd shake my hand and wish me well,"
Yarber said. "Then he started telling me about his offense."

Erickson told Yarber that in the Idaho spread offense he
might catch fifty, sixty, seventy balls a year, that he could
play immediately and become a true focal point of the offense; he could be a team leader and have a chance to play
on a championship team and be the Most Valuable Player
in the Big Sky Conference.

"He made another point I couldn't deny," Yarber said.
"He told me, 'Scouts will come to Illinois and Purdue, but
they won't be coming to see the guy who caught twenty-five
passes, they'll be coming to see those other guys, but who

knows? Maybe you'll catch their attention.' He said, 'If you come to Idaho, NFL scouts will come to see you, they'll have to see you because of the numbers you'll put up.'"

Yarber—now at UCLA on Jim Mora's staff—is one of the most respected recruiters and wide receivers coaches in the country. He credits much of his inspiration to Erickson. "Everything he told me was true," Yarber said. "I mean, every little detail; I caught a lot of passes [seventy-five in 1985], the scouts came to see me, I went to the Redskins and played in a Super Bowl. What more can you ask?"

Building the offensive system required players and Erickson, who had a remarkable capacity to spot the specific skills he desired for this offense, was the right guy to find those players. They opened the 1982 season in Spokane against heavily favored Washington State. Erickson believed they could beat the Cougars and preached to his team exactly what needed to happen for the upset to occur.

"The final score [a 34–14 loss] was a little deceiving," Gilbertson said. "It was really closer than that, but the big thing was, everything Dennis talked about that we needed to do was played out on the field. We had a couple defensive breakdowns on things he had stressed all week, but it was one of those weird games. We lost, but we believed; that stuff happens sometimes. We were playing this crazy-ass football, but we could have won the damn game and everyone on our team knew it. That first game, even though we lost, made believers out of every player we had."

The Vandals roared through the season with two four-game win streaks and finished 9-4, the season ending on a Division I-AA quarterfinal loss to Eastern Kentucky in Richmond, Kentucky. They played a road game at Northern Iowa early in the season that Gilbertson still remembers.

"I don't know if they never saw film of us or what," he said,

> but there we were, a long ways from home, playing at their place and they seemed to have no idea what to do against the spread. They would stay in their base defense with their middle linebacker watching us run routes around him, you know, doing what he was told. We had receivers uncovered and wide open all day. I mean, this was a first-year coach full of piss and vinegar and we could have had as many points as we wanted—literally, we could have had eighty—but Dennis could see they weren't ready so we got enough to win the game and he backed off the throttle [in a 38–13 win].

Erickson's four years at Idaho commenced the most successful string of football seasons in school history. He was 32-15 in that time; Idaho was 113-45 from '82 through '94 with the spread offense under head coaches Erickson, Keith Gilbertson, and Gregg Smith. The fewest wins for an Erickson team at Idaho came in his third season, when the Vandals were 6-5, but one of those victories for the Division I-AA program was significant. It came against Oregon State, coached by Joe Avezzano.

Idaho beat the Beavers 41–22, but it wasn't just the result that made an impression on Oregon State athletic director Dee Andros, it was the manner in which it was achieved. As old school as they come, Andros was an Oklahoma Marine who fought for a month in Iwo Jima, lived to tell about it, and came back to play for Bud Wilkinson's legendary postwar Oklahoma Sooners. Andros knew what commitment looked like on a football team, knew about accountability and respect for teammates as well as any coach in the country.

As a head coach at Idaho, then later at Oregon State, Andros was a bare-knuckled running-game coach whose teams were led by fullbacks and middle linebackers. They considered it a great day if they could beat you 3–0 in the mud, which they did one day in Corvallis to a No. 1 USC team that featured O. J. Simpson.

But that day years later in Idaho as Oregon State athletic director, Andros saw the future of college football.

10

Settling In and Getting Out
(Late 1980s, Early 1990s)

The last thing Sam Jankovich wanted was for the coach of his national championship football team to walk out five months after bringing home a title, but in retrospect, the timing couldn't have been better. The new Miami athletic director, still in his first year on the job, had enough time to call some old pals in the profession for coaching references after Schnellenberger's hasty and ill-planned departure, before Jankovich headed off to the annual college coaches convention in Dallas.

Organized by Dallas Cowboys college scouting director Gil Brandt, the event was, and remains, a one-stop job fair for football coaches and athletic directors looking for football coaches. Basketball coaches have their own job mart in conjunction with the Final Four tournament, but for football coaches, Dallas was the ultimate schmoozing, grazing, and networking site. Jankovich went there with an interest in talking to John Cooper, who was then building a successful program at the University of Tulsa. He was also interested in Jimmy Johnson, who had managed, against such major obstacles as having only fifty scholarships as a result of NCAA violations, to get the Oklahoma State program pointed in the right direction. Jankovich had friends who knew Cooper well, which made him the prime object in his search, but he wanted to learn more about Johnson.

As soon as he arrived, Jankovich was steered away from Johnson by Brandt and Associated Press writer Herschel Nissenson. Separately, each of them warned that Johnson was riding high at Oklahoma State, having just successfully recruited a potentially great running back named Thurman Thomas, and he'd be nuts to leave what he had built up in Stillwater to be the one to follow the guy who had just won a national championship at Miami.

Boy, were they wrong.

Jankovich was about to get on an elevator at the Hyatt Regency, where the meetings were being held, when the doors opened and out walked Jimmy Johnson. "I said hi to him and we chatted for a few minutes," Jankovich said of the unexpected conversation. "I told him I was thinking about John Cooper for our vacancy, that I was going to be going out to dinner with John that night, and I was wondering if Jimmy had any thoughts about John he wanted to share with me. Jimmy said, 'What the hell, I'm a better coach than John Cooper and I like the water.'"

Jankovich was smitten. He loved Johnson's self-confidence and sociable manner and, based on what he had heard from Nissenson and Brandt, that he was a good recruiter. Jankovich went to dinner with Cooper as planned and then met Johnson back at his hotel room that same night. If he were dating, Jankovich would have been two-timing, but this was no simple date, this was a marriage proposal. He and Johnson met again the next morning for breakfast and again that night.

"I went to Nissenson and Brandt and said, 'Either you guys are nuts or I'm a total idiot because I talked to this guy and I think he's interested; I think I could offer him the job and he'd take it and not even have much of a discussion about money,'" Jankovich said. "They said, 'You're kidding,' and I said they should both talk to him. Each one of them came back to me and said, 'You're right, he wants it.'"

Jankovich had Johnson agreeing to a contract two days after they bumped into each other at the elevator. To the athletic director, it seemed a great hire; Johnson was young and energetic, solid as they come on the defensive side of the ball. But his arrival in Miami was uncomfortable, at best.

The local favorite for the job was Tom Olivadotti, the defensive coordinator for Schnellenberger's 1983 national champions. Schnellenberger left behind a talented staff of assistants, a group that very much impressed Jankovich. In his book *Turning the Thing Around*, Johnson wrote, "One of my biggest concerns about taking the job was that Sam demanded whoever replaced Schnellenberger retain his old staff."

Jankovich remembers it differently. "I never demanded anything," Jankovich said. "I told Jimmy, 'You have to keep some of these coaches, meaning these are good coaches.' One of the smartest things Jimmy did was he kept Joe Brodsky, he kept Gary Stevens, Herbert Alexander, and when he kept that offensive staff together, that really allowed Jimmy to concentrate on the defensive side—his area of expertise—and on special teams and those guys were with Jimmy that entire time."

Johnson's first introduction to the staff sounds like something out of a movie. Olivadotti had a bundle of car keys on the table in front of him and kept lifting them and dropping them on the table, each clashing noise drawing more attention to him as Johnson tried to talk to the coaches. In his book, Johnson wrote that Olivadotti told him, "I can't coach defense the way your teams play defense." There was no question the two of them didn't get along, presumably because Olivadotti thought he'd get the job Johnson had.

But Johnson's book doesn't explain that Olivadotti left

and Johnson's associate Butch Davis came in to coach the defense that first season, staying for four more years after that. Jankovich's "demands" didn't turn out to be so binding after all. "He brought in Butch, he let Olivadotti go, I didn't force anybody down his throat," Jankovich said. "The only one he kept that hurt him was Bill Trout, he wasn't a J. J. guy."

Trout was the defensive assistant in the booth for Johnson during the infamous—for Miami—Boston College game, the last regular-season game in Johnson's first full year, when Doug Flutie threw a Hail Mary touchdown pass to Gerald Phelan on the last play of the game. Trout had informed Johnson he would be resigning after the game, and Johnson later wrote that he was told Trout had left the press box before the Flutie pass play. In any case, the Miami secondary badly misplayed the pass by breaking the proverbial cardinal sin in those situations, allowing Phelan—the deepest receiver—to slip behind all Hurricanes defenders.

It wasn't the kind of first season Johnson or Jankovich had hoped for, but 8-5 wasn't terrible, and it was an improvement over Schnellenberger's first year. What griped Johnson the most was that Miami was 2-0 with home games against Maryland and Boston College to close out the regular season and they lost each of them in gut-wrenching fashion, 42–40 to Maryland after blowing a 31–0 halftime lead before the classic last-play collapse against BC. They then flew to Tempe, Arizona, where they were defeated by UCLA 39–37 on a last-minute field goal in the Fiesta Bowl. It wasn't good. Miami hadn't lost as many games since Schnellenberger's first year, and Johnson wasn't about to accept the status quo.

After he finished four years at Idaho with the four most productive teams in school history, Erickson got a Division I offer. He took a radical makeover job at Wyoming, where he turned a wishbone program inside out and successfully converted it to the spread during his first season, finishing second nationally in passing yardage in 1986. Then came the call from Washington State, almost a second home by then.

Leaving after a year wasn't going to go well, but Pullman was different, that was a home base, a destination job that Wyoming never was. That and the fact that WSU was offering him $60,000 allowed him to make a quick decision.

When he settled into his office as the new Cougars head coach in 1987, Dennis Erickson's career appeared to have arrived at home, or maybe in the end zone. He was in a place that had a reputation for turning enthusiastic beginnings into leaden expeditions for football coaches in the major conference in the western United States, where virtually all other schools held advantages of population, resources, or geography — or all three — over WSU. In terms of proximity to metropolitan recruiting centers, even Oregon State University had the advantage of being as close to Seattle as Pullman, and it was much closer to greater Portland and the rich talent grounds of Northern California.

For Erickson, Pullman was what he had always wanted; it seemed that, in his third job in three years, his run to find the right fit had finally ended. The day after the announcement was made on January 8, 1987, the lead story in the *Spokane Spokesman-Review* quoted the thirty-nine-year-old coach saying it had been "a gut-wrenching decision" to leave Wyoming after just one season, but "my goal in life and in coaching was to be the head football coach at Washington State. I was raised a Cougar," Erickson said in the story written by Dan Weaver. "My father coached here. I coached here. I played [at Montana State] for a man named Jim Sweeney who had a lot to do with Washington State football over the years."

At the end of the 1986 season, Erickson also got interest from Wisconsin. They were stunned by Wyoming's spread offense, which left Camp Randall Stadium shaken after a 21–12 victory over the Badgers. In one year Erickson had taken a 3-8 wishbone team to a 6-6 record behind a spread offense that finished second in the nation in passing and was tied for the national lead with thirty aerial touchdowns. The Big 10 was clearly an upgrade over Wyoming, but Erickson was a Northwest guy, not a Midwest guy, and he eventually declined the offer. Three weeks later Washington State athletic director Dick Young offered him the job at the NCAA and American Football Coaches Association convention in San Diego. He accepted, but word leaked out before he had a chance to fly back to Wyoming and inform the players.

During his time as head coach at nearby Idaho, Erickson had been as popular in Pullman as a backup quarterback on a losing team. Erickson's team won two conference titles and advanced to the I-AA playoffs twice in his four years at Idaho, the first stretch of four years in school history in which the football team had not had at least one losing season. While Washington State was 20-23-1 under Walden from 1982 to 1985, Idaho, covered by the same newspapers, was 32-15 for Erickson, with a passing offense that put up a record number of points and offensive statistics.

When he arrived in Pullman, Erickson quickly realized that while it may have been his dream job, he was starting out with a nightmarish roster than included only six seniors on scholarship. At his news conference the day after the announcement, reporters reminded Erickson that his first two opponents that fall, in order, were against Sweeney's Fresno State team, followed by Wyoming. "God help us all," Erickson told the *Spokesman-Review*.

The talent Walden left behind was painfully young as well as having been recruited to fit an option-based rushing offense. Had Walden stayed, it would have appropriately been considered another rebuilding year, though the Cougars had been just 3-7-1 in 1986 and a combined 7-14-1 in the two previous seasons. Walden had recruited two good running backs—Steve Broussard and Richard Calvin—and a quarterback with a linebacker's mentality, Timm Rosenbach. The youth and inexperience made 1987 a season of low expectations for Walden's, Erickson's, or anyone else's system.

This was a different kind of test than Wyoming, where the wishbone offense had been beaten down and everyone was eager for something new. At Pullman, the perennial underdog mentality was wearing thin and the question was whether the Cougars' talent, such as it was, could match up with anybody at the Pac-10 level. For as much as Erickson had always dreamed of coaching Washington State one day, he could hardly have walked in at a worse time to unveil a new system.

Rosenbach, son of a WSU athletic department official and former high school coach, had been a standout prep quarterback in Pullman and was placed at the position because his athleticism fit the role. His pugnacious personality was more typical of defensive players. Still, he was the sophomore quarterback in 1987 for an offense geared to run, and he looked the part.

Personnel dictated that Erickson could introduce the spread offense only in bits and pieces when he could get away with it. Most of the time, Washington State used two backs in a more conventional offensive set based on the available talent. Broussard was the leading receiver in the Pac-10 that season, which said something about Erickson's offensive creativity under duress.

The season started with a relief after wins at home over Fresno State and Coach Sweeney, 41–24, and Wyoming, by a final count of 43-28. The next week at Michigan produced the first predictable loss in what became a 3-7-1 season.

"It was all about matchups," Rosenbach recalled of that game. "When we played at Michigan, we were in our one-back stuff the whole first half and we had guys running uncovered through the defense. Michigan wasn't used to seeing the spread or seeing a back coming out of the backfield in motion, so things were open and they didn't know how to cover it." Schemes are good for a while, but turnovers and overwhelming talent have a way of winning more often than not, and that was the case in the second half, when Michigan carved out a 44–18 win before an Ann Arbor crowd of 103,521.

Michigan coach Bo Schembechler later dismissed it with a backhanded compliment. "I was amazed by what you did with that gimmick offense," he told Erickson after the game, a thought often expressed by other coaches, though usually not to Erickson's face. Schembechler might more accurately have described it as an offense for which he was unable to make adequate preparations in the first half, when Washington State held a lead.

By the end of the season Rosenbach was beaten up physically and disillusioned emotionally. He wanted out. He finished the season having thrown eleven touchdowns and twenty-four interceptions, including five against Oregon State and four each against Arizona State and Washington.

Erickson's offense appeared to be coming undone, exposed by playing in a major conference with a team that was sorely lacking for talent. There were also issues at home that involved Marilyn, who had developed an ulcer after death threats were called in to the house phone following her husband's decision to leave Wyoming and an incident when disgruntled fans let the family's new puppy out of the yard, allowing it to run away.

During that first season at wsu in 1987, Marilyn's ulcer was raging. On the morning of October 24—the date of the home game against Arizona — she collapsed on the bathroom floor, was found spitting up blood moments later, and taken to the emergency room. At the hospital she was admitted to a room she surprisingly shared with Bill Moos, an athletic department employee who had been shot in the face that morning by a booster in a quail-hunting party. Moos, the current athletic director at Washington State, lost vision in an eye, Marilyn recovered in time, and that afternoon the Cougars went out and won their only Pacific-10 Conference game all season, a 45–28 romp over Arizona.

That game offered a glimmer of hope for the future, but the futures of Erickson, the school's football program, and the spread offense were all in doubt in January 1988 when Rosenbach walked into Erickson's office and announced his intention to become a linebacker. Rosenbach told Erickson he wasn't suited to play quarterback in the offense and wanted to be switched to defense for the good of the team. The vocal cynics at Washington State were pointing out to all who would listen that Erickson's hot-damn offense was 9-3 in 1985 at I-AA Idaho, then 6-6 at mid-major Wyoming, and 3-7-1 at Washington State. The higher the level Erickson coached, the worse the record his new offense generated, and now, with a year's work into it, his quarterback wanted out.

At that moment in 1988, the chance of the spread offense gaining traction nationally and becoming a force of change in college football would have got you immeasurably long odds at Las Vegas. Had Rosenbach switched positions and a new quarterback been brought in to start all over, it all might have ended right there in Pullman, Washington, in 1988.

Instead, the approaching 1988 season took on an almost mythical quality for the manner in which obstacles thrown at them were overcome, one after another, in stunning fashion. It started with Erickson challenging Rosenbach's doubts. He told his rising junior quarterback that he hadn't yet committed to being the best he could be and because of that he was indecisive in games, creating self-doubt and increasing the chance for poor decisions that result in interceptions. The coach saw the potential but thought Rosenbach's lack of confidence was betraying him. Erickson told Rosenbach he needed to make a decision about who he wanted to be.

"He said my teammates would help me, that I had to be accountable for my position and trust in them," Rosenbach recalled. The small-group cohesion approach instilled in Erickson by his father was on the line, and it worked. By the time he got to spring football drills, Rosenbach had made up his mind to be a quarterback.

First he listened, then he tried to follow what Erickson suggested, and then things started getting better. He didn't turn the ball over as much in spring drills. He was making better decisions and gradually figuring out what was happening around him on offense and defense.

"I began to realize where the weaknesses were and that's one of the things Dennis was great at," Rosenbach said.

He never over-coached me, he was a guy that put me into situations and let me figure them out myself. His approach gave me a way to make my own decisions, not just react; you end up being accountable for the offense, thinking on your feet a little bit as you go.

You could say after our discussions that off-season, I heard him in a different way. He told me there were going to be receivers open all over the field and I should start by hitting the first guy who came open. He was right, we did have guys open everywhere. We built on that.

Having done it himself, Erickson had a special knack for telling quarterbacks just what they needed to hear without overloading them with too much information. "It would be easier for a coach to demand specific decisions in certain circumstances, but when you do that, you remove a quarter-back's ability to take responsibility for the offense and lead the team, and that's what you're after," Rosenbach said. "I was too dumb to realize [it] at the time, but he was basical-ly handing me the opportunity to be a leader.

"He explained enough for me to get a grip on the concept without overwhelming me with a bunch of technical stuff; we sat in the film room and went over game situations, one after the other. He'd say, 'What are you seeing here? What happens to the linebacker if this receiver goes deep right here?'

"He'd give you one or two things and he'd let you figure out the rest, he let you take ownership."

Rosenbach's confidence spilled over to his teammates, and his linebacker mentality helped him grow from an unsure and mistake-prone player into a natural team leader in just a few months. Washington State didn't turn the game inside out in that 1988 season, but the buzz following Erickson was attracting a lot of attention in the coaching fraternity.

In the off-season between 1987 and 1988, Texas Chris-tian University coach Jim Wacker brought his entire staff to Pullman to observe what was taking place in the Cougars' offense. Fifty years after TCU's Davey O'Brien became the first player to win the Heisman Trophy and the Camp and Maxwell Awards in the same year—operating out of an of-fense his coach called the "Meyer spread"—the 1988 TCU staff traveled to Washington State to learn about this new offense that came to be recognized as the spread.

"People were just calling it the one-back," said Noel Maz-zone, TCU's quarterback coach at the time,

and there were some parallels to what [Washington State] had been doing at the time and what we had been doing. [WSU] was in the split-back veer with [previous coach] Jim Walden and we had been doing some veer, trying to make things happen, but everyone was talking about the one-back and we wanted to learn more.

Dennis was doing a lot of motion-to-empty stuff out of the shotgun and that was something not a lot of people were doing, actually I don't know that anyone else was doing that, but it was innovative and we were trying to stay ahead of people, but the truth is, that motion stuff, the empty stuff? It's pretty much exactly what everyone's doing now, what, thirty-some years later.

With his first season behind him, Jimmy Johnson used the spring 1985 offseason to make Miami football more of his own program. He told reporters he was stabbed in the back by some of the assistant coaches he let go, so he brought in new ones with whom he had a better relationship. It was all calculated for effect, but this was how the former psychology major from the University of Arkansas began working his way into players' heads. He would challenge them to verbalize what they wanted for themselves in years to come and then direct all their attention back to their present situation; the aspiration, the urgent importance of getting better and demanding the same from teammates on a daily basis, was Johnson's skillful approach.

He was one of those white coaches, like the one who would follow him, who got along exceptionally well with black players. He sought them out, talked to them in ways that were relevant to them, and encouraged them to be themselves. He liked the outward shows of emotion, the chest-thumping exhortations that were more commonly seen in the NFL.

Trouble was, this was the NCAA's game and it didn't appreciate the hip-hop-fueled approach. It eventually ended the Hurricanes' on-field antics with binding legislation in the form of an umbrella rule designed specifically for Miami that also happened to cover everyone else.

It is Rule 9, Section 2, Article 1 in the NCAA rulebook, originated decades earlier but updated out of necessity in 1987. It is the section that contains the unsportsmanlike conduct rule that started out restricting celebrations and the removal of helmets while on the field of play and was expanded to include penalties for what was considered to be taunting. It was more commonly known as the Miami Rule, meaning the Jimmy Johnson Hurricanes of 1985 and '86.

The Miami players' aggressive style attracted attention and caused great consternation for the school's president, who wasn't prepared to accept that it was all an unintended consequence of a master plan to make Miami a national powerhouse in football. The 'Canes came to symbolize the role of unwanted trendsetters in sports, though they were far from the only ones who pulled off their helmets, bowed in the end zone, or raised their arms to the heavens after big plays. The difference was that Miami blew on the scene seemingly out of thin air, disrupting the more structured order of college football's traditional winners. And yes, they had a number of high-profile black players. It wasn't the kind of thing you ever saw out of Woody Hayes's Ohio State Buckeyes, Bo Schembechler's Michigan Wolverines, or Bear Bryant's Alabama Crimson Tide.

They were symbols to much of white America that the Joe College game fans knew not so long ago, played by thick-necked frat boys who might have grown up next door, had been taken over by bigger, faster players who ritualized their celebrations, of which there were many, and had no problem telling the opposition it was going to get beat, then reminding them of that when the deed was done. It is instructive about the culture that while several of the standout players at Miami were white, from Jim Kelly early on to Rusty

Meadaris to Vinny Testaverde later, the swaggering style was almost always associated with the black players, sometimes using code words that implied more than they said. Television analysts would often mention the "Miami style" when Michael Irvin, Melvin Bratton, or Warren Sapp was pictured in celebration, but if it was Bernie Kosar, Dan Sileo, or Gino Torretta, broadcasters usually referred to as "excitement" or fulfilling a necessary role as a "team motivator."

When the 'Canes arrived, they wanted everyone to know they were in the house, and in that they were wholly successful. Miami built the most dominant college football program of the '80s and early '90s with players recruited for the most part from South Florida who stood distinctly apart from what the nation had come to expect from its football powers in the South.

Miami's transition from an all-white team to a team made up mostly of African Americans and other minorities occurred gradually, kicking in with Schnellenberger's 1983 recruiting class and going full-speed ahead when Jimmy Johnson was hired to replace him.

Jim Dent wrote a book — *The Junction Boys* — about Bryant's legendary Texas A&M offseason camp, but those who saw the Schnellenberger era at Miami are convinced that what the 'Canes went through was tougher than anything the Aggies knew. The players couldn't practice too hard, or so it seemed, an attribute that would put any football coach in a courageously competitive state of mind, and that sense of outworking everyone to gain a physically intimidating edge became, to those within the program, the defining aspect of Miami Hurricane football.

Johnson's second season was much smoother. His staff was in place and the 'Canes, behind new quarterback Vinny Testaverde, rolled to a 10-2 record, losing only their first game to Florida and their last game to Tennessee, in the Sugar Bowl.

It was the next year, Johnson's third, that burnished an image of Miami football that seemed to insult America's sense of propriety in competitive athletics.

Miami had its best season since the national championship of 1983, winning eleven straight games, including a 28–16 whipping of Oklahoma when the Hurricanes were ranked No. 2 and the Sooners, with flamboyant, outspoken linebacker Brian Bosworth, were ranked No. 1. It was Bosworth, who is white, who spent most of the week before the game talking about the renegade 'Canes, and it was Miami that took most of the national abuse before winning the game.

At the end of the season there was another No. 1 vs. No. 2 matchup, only this time Miami was the top-ranked team, playing what the country was led to believe was the personification of middle-class American, blue-collar college football, Penn State and coach Joe Paterno. The Fiesta Bowl in Tempe, Arizona, was portrayed as the clean-cut kids against the thugs. The narrative was enhanced by Miami players deplaning on arrival dressed in combat fatigues, just as the Washington Redskins had done in 1983 when they arrived in Pasadena for Super Bowl XVII prior to defeating, oddly enough, Miami.

One of Miami's leaders, defensive tackle Dan Sileo, took credit for coming up with the fatigues concept. Maybe the 'Canes remembered that Redskins moment, maybe they were encouraged by Sileo, but this time the combat team didn't get the job done after one of quarterback Vinny Testaverde's worst college games resulted in a 14–10 loss—and the loss of the national title—to Penn State.

It wasn't the game that America seemed to remember as much as the image of Miami players wearing combat fatigues and the incident that happened at a bowl-sponsored steak fry that was supposed to involve both teams and coaches. Instead of a full contingent, just a few Penn State players showed up, and Paterno didn't bother to come. Miami players were not amused by an attempt at humor from a Penn State player who said his school was supposed to be lily white, but he pointed out they had black players, too. "On occasion," the player said, "we even let our black players sit down at the table and eat with us."

The 'Canes were not laughing. Jerome Brown stepped to the microphone and said, "We didn't sit down to dinner with the Japanese the night before Pearl Harbor and we're not going to get up here and act like a bunch of monkeys to entertain you people. We're going to war."

With that, Brown, his teammates, and the Miami coaches walked out. Most accounts of the incident skipped over the racist comment from the Penn State player and settled on the disruptive departure of the Miami players. The image was set, and losing the game the next day only served to delight most fans outside of South Florida.

The very next year Miami won a second national championship, the first for Jimmy Johnson, matching Schnellenberger. On this occasion the game was played in the Orange Bowl, Miami was No. 2, Oklahoma was No. 1, and the 'Canes won it, 20–14.

A year later Johnson coached Miami to an 11-1 record, losing only to Lou Holtz and Notre Dame on the road. A few months after finishing No. 2 in the national polls, Johnson took an offer he couldn't refuse from an old college friend named Jerry Jones and went off to coach the Dallas Cowboys. Just like that, Miami AD Sam Jankovich had to find someone who could not just continue but improve on what had become the new national power in college football.

In his book *God's Coach*, about Cowboys' coach Tom Landry, Skip Bayless wrote that Jones called Johnson during Miami's season, told him he was thinking about buying the team, and asked if Johnson would come along to Dallas as his coach if it could all be worked out. "That might have happened," said Gil Brandt, the longtime Cowboys' personnel man. "It might not have. Nobody [connected to the Cowboys' previous ownership] knew anything about what was going on back then. There was no due diligence in the sale of the team, it was all cloaked in secrecy."

Whether Johnson was coaching the last half of that season while expecting to leave Miami with a verbal agreement from the Cowboys or not, he departed quickly, in a huff, not unlike the departure of his predecessor. Miami's administration had a contentious relationship with its football coaches in the 1980s, having gone from a small private school about to eliminate football to one where power was increasingly vested in the coach and his players. Jankovich was thoroughly enmeshed in university administration and very much admired for the work he had done to bring more money to the school through athletics, but Foote and others felt they were too often put on the spot when asked to explain some of the indiscrete actions by members of the football team that were held up as a bad example of the direction in which collegiate athletics had turned. Foote wanted a Harvard of the South at Miami and Johnson's politically incorrect football team wasn't what he had in mind. The school president was delighted by the wins but embarrassed by the actions of the Hurricanes.

From the time Schnellenberger started in 1979 — with a 5-6 record — through the 1988 season, Miami posted a record of 93-25 with two national championships. When Johnson left for the Cowboys, the University of Miami had been 23-1-0 with a national championship in his last two seasons. So when Johnson headed out, Foote's message to Jankovich was simple enough. He wanted to win just like they had been winning, but he wanted the bad reviews to stop. No more embarrassments.

11

Changes, Even in the South (1990s)

The coach who first conceptualized the potential of an all-out passing assault—a concept different from the one Swarthout considered in the rebuilt T formation—may have been Don Coryell, yet another Northwest guy. Coryell was from Seattle, attended the University of Washington, and later developed the deep-passing game at San Diego State University before moving on to a long and wildly entertaining professional coaching career. Coryell's philosophies informed coaches like Bill Walsh, John Madden, and Joe Gibbs. His instrumental role in using all parts of the field in the passing game and finding ways for smaller receivers to contribute wasn't always recognized because of the relative lack of attention he got at San Diego State.

But even Coryell's influence didn't flow from west to east in a grand wave, though many southern college offenses, such as Alabama's when Bear Bryant coached Joe Namath, used chapters from the Coryell playbook. Had Coryell, an army paratrooper in World War II, come out of the service and landed for some reason in, say, Georgia, Florida, or Alabama and started his coaching career from one of those locations in college, the game may well have gone airborne much sooner. Football coaches are no different than professionals in any line of work: when they see success, they are drawn to copy the blueprint for themselves.

"I don't like that term *copycat*," said Atlanta Falcons head coach Mike Smith when asked about the wildcat formation — in which a running back takes a direct snap from the center — that found its way into NFL playbooks in recent years. "I think of it as fishing off a long pier. If you're there, and you're not getting any bites, but you look down at the end of the pier and see some guy reeling them in, you're going to head down that way, aren't you? That's just being smart."

By any name or phrase, it's an observable fact that football coaches will run from whatever long-held truths they preached to their teams about offensive theory when they find something that works better than what they have.

Had Dennis Erickson stayed at Washington State after the 1988 season, or maybe taken another job somewhere else on the West Coast a few years later, the spread would have eventually moved to the Midwest, back east, and down south, but it would not have proliferated as rapidly had he not been hired to coach national power Miami in 1989. From there, the offense exploded like a keg of dynamite on college football's center stage. This wasn't Pullman anymore.

College football in the South was at least a full decade behind the West Coast in terms of the passing game, owing to the holdover from segregated football in the region, when all-white teams routinely slugged it out against other all-white teams. Only after rosters in the South were more integrated with a wider variety of athletic talents did exploration of the passing game begin in earnest, albeit gradually. It came from the West, most notably through the friendship between University of Southern California coach John McKay and Alabama's Bryant. They met in an airport bar in 1969 and planned a home-and-home series in succeeding years, with the first game to be played in 1970 in Birmingham, where Bryant knew McKay's team, with a talented load of black players, would show the southern crowd the future of football.

USC won handily, Bryant's point was made, and the South opened its doors to integrated football. The truth is that Bryant was about the last Southeastern Conference coach to populate his team with black players, a consequence of living in a state with prevailing prejudice led by Governor George Wallace, who built a career of support from white racist groups such as the Ku Klux Klan.

With a bureaucratic pace that didn't unduly distress their fans, southern teams began opening their playbooks and rosters to accommodate the talent that was emerging in southern classrooms and football fields. When they upgraded talent with African American players, southern schools began opening the offense with more passing and more effective running games. They didn't have to resort to only the "tough little runts" approach from Bryant or the limitations of the triple option.

Veteran coaches who knew only integration in the South can remember what it was like before the spread and how it affected the game. Kevin Steele was a young assistant coach at Tennessee in the 1980s, breaking down opponents' game film, assigned the task of making cutups from reels of offensive plays for upcoming opponents, one of which was LSU. It was a package of four games that comprised about 125 plays. That was football in the South before the spread. Against Tennessee, Steele recalls LSU lining up out of two personnel groupings the entire game.

"In one, they had two tight ends, two backs, and one receiver and in the other they had one tight end, two receivers, and two backs; their base personnel grouping was a tight end, two backs, and two receivers and they had a total of six formations, mostly I-pro and I-slot," Steele said.

"The thing I distinctly remember is that they had eight motions; eight plays out of about 125 when someone would be in motion. It was a different world, man."

This was the mid-1980s. It was the way college football was played in the South while Erickson was emptying backfields and sending out five receivers for thick linebackers to sort out and determine which ones to cover. It was a different world, man.

Tennessee wasn't much different, until a new offensive coach brought some foreign concepts that were a source of irritation for Steele in spring drills in 1988. After his time cutting up film at Tennessee, Steele spent a year at New Mexico State and three at Oklahoma State before returning to Tennessee in 1987, the year before Walt Harris joined the staff as the offensive coordinator.

Harris had come from Illinois, off the staff of Mike White, and was steeped in the growth of California passing offenses in the 1970s. He had been an offensive assistant at Stanford where the quarterback was Jim Plunkett, and then, in six years as head coach at California, White's quarterbacks included three classic West Coast drop-back passers, Steve Bartkowski, Vince Ferragamo, and Joe Roth. White won a Pacific-8 Conference championship in 1975 on a Cal team that included running back Chuck Muncie, receiver Wesley Walker, and Roth. This was a Big Boy passing game, West Coast style, with motion and tight ends who could catch the ball running hard on a dig route against your middle linebacker.

Harris absorbed much of White's approach, having been raised in San Francisco on the T formation, then later I formation passing offenses. He was on the Illinois staff that won the Big 10 Conference in 1983 when White was named UPI coach of the year—it was the first team to beat every other conference opponent in a single season. White and Harris were not involved with the spread, but they had picked up on one of its major component parts—motion, and lots of it.

"That was the first time I had ever seen a lot of motion," Steele said. "It was the first time I had seen people break the huddle, get the tight end down in a stance, back him off the line, and then send him in motion. I was like, 'Daggone, we can't even play football in practice anymore? We gotta spend all our time on motion adjustments?' We were fuss-in' as defensive coaches, I remember that from that first day with Walt Harris on the staff."

In the South everyone used to try to keep pace with Bry-ant at Alabama, a man who constructed a Hall of Fame coaching career by building tough teams with tough people, making them work for everything they got in practice and in games. For all his image of being an old-school coach, Bryant was a fisherman on a long pier, just like the rest of them. He had been a straightforward power football coach who was willing to pass the ball around some when he had a quar-terback named Joe Namath. Then he ditched his straight-ahead, old-school offense for the wishbone, junked that for a more open passing attack, and had he lived longer he may well have recruited players fit to run a spread offense.

For Steele and a lot of coaches in the South, Washington State's lopsided victory at Tennessee in 1988 was a transcen-dent milepost in the game. "We had heard about the West Coast approach where they'd throw it thirty or thirty-five times a game, but that wasn't what we did," Steele said. "I think we figured that was another part of the country that played the game another way and we weren't going to pay much attention to it; not that it was wrong or anything, it just wasn't what we did where I came from, so there was no point in getting too wrapped up in it.

"I remember Georgia Tech coming to Neyland Stadium one time and throwing two passes the entire game, no big deal," he said. "Now we're seeing this team running through us like it's playday or something, with people in motion, crossing routes, no backs. You knew then this stuff wasn't going away; it was a nightmare to prepare for."

Despite the doom and gloom expressed by the dead-ender fans, most were supportive that off-season between Erickson's first and second years in Pullman. This was Washington State and they knew the difficulties of building a program. Most of the fans, like those who attended a Washington State fund-raiser golf tournament in Pasco, Washington, in the summer of '88, were enthusiastic and encouraging.

Erickson was the main attraction at the golf outing with Timm's father Lynn Rosenbach, trainer Jim Bartko, and Moos. It was an experimental fund-raiser in Central Washington Rosenbach had organized to bring Cougar fans together in that part of the state and Erickson was the draw.

Lynn Rosenbach was a former football coach at Olympic Junior College, a ferry-boat ride west of Seattle, who was now in battle against cancer that had already claimed an arm. Rosenbach, who had also coached at Montana on Jack Swarthout's staff, remained incredibly active in the athletic department, transferring those locker room coaching skills into strategies to build the Cougars' fan base.

Coming back from the Pasco golf outing in the university van, the foursome stopped in Washtucna, a town of two hundred or so named after a Palouse Indian chief in the scablands of eastern Washington. There isn't a lot to do in the town of that size unless you happen to need a rest stop and a beer. They parked at a tavern just off I-26, the east-west two-lane road that takes you to Colfax, then up the hill to Pullman.

Moos and Rosenbach went to the restroom while Erickson and Bartko ordered four longneck Bud Lights. Moos was congratulating Rosenbach for his efforts in establishing the successful golf tournament and remembers Rosenbach coughing in the bathroom as he walked out. After taking longer than he should have, Rosenbach finally came out in a hurry, slapped Moos on the shoulder twice sharply, and said in a rushed tone, "Gotta go." Moos saw a look of serious concern in Rosenbach's eyes. Erickson threw some money on the counter and they all ran to the van.

It was fifty miles to the nearest hospital in Colfax, but the winding, two-lane road made it at least an hour's drive at any other time. Bartko hopped behind the wheel, Moos sat next to him, and Erickson positioned himself next to Rosenbach on the bench seat in back.

The old van may have never gone so fast for so long, dipping under 90 mph only on the tightest turns as Rosenbach began coughing up blood while Erickson delivered the pep talk of his life. "You stay with us Lynn, goddammit," Erickson said. "You're gonna be okay, you're going to make it, we're gonna get you taken care of, just hang with me, man." Sweating and gasping for breath, Rosenbach spit up more and more blood and Erickson would mop it up, alternately consoling and encouraging his quarterback's father.

Bartko slammed the van to a stop at the hospital emergency entrance in Colfax and Erickson threw back a balky handle on the side door, kicked it open, and carried Rosenbach out. After a few minutes in the emergency room, with doctors inserting needles and talking about pumps, Moos excused himself to call Rosenbach's wife in Pullman, twenty-five minutes away, telling her to get in her car and drive down the hill to Colfax as soon as she could.

Erickson stayed with Rosenbach the whole time, holding his hands, mopping a feverish forehead, wiping blood off the Washington State golf shirt he wore with his name tag still on his left breast. Moos came back from the phone call as Erickson walked out of the emergency room, his chest heaving to take in gulps of oxygen, his face streaked with tears. "We lost him," Erickson said.

Minutes later Rosenbach's wife and son arrived. Moos was the first to meet them and break the news that a cancerous tumor had ruptured an aorta. When they went to the room, Erickson was there, silent, head bowed, at the bedside.

Not a lot of people nationally were watching the separate paths of Miami and Washington State football in 1988, but Sam Jankovich didn't miss a thing. He knew what it took to build a team like Erickson had in 1988 at Washington State and he was fascinated by the thought of what Erickson's offense might be capable of at Miami.

The selection of Johnson's successor was his call as the athletic director, but Jankovich knew the arc of his career would ride on the wisdom of his choice. "The president and I had an understanding about hiring of coaches—it was going to be my call—and yes, it got ugly," Jankovich recalled.

Though he had hired the popular Johnson, Jankovich was still perceived by many South Floridians as an outsider, but there was a different perception of him inside the university. A decisive administrator, Jankovich understood how to raise money. When he started at Miami, annual donations to the athletic department generated about $750,000, but they would increase to more than $3 million after the 1989 season. That sort of financial deliverance buys confidence with university decision makers.

With South Florida newspapers, sports talk radio yakkers, and players constantly making the case for Gary Stevens, Jankovich was increasingly seen as the guy who might ruin it all by not hiring everyone's favorite. Returning quarter-back Steve Walsh suggested in the daily prints that he might pass on his senior season if Stevens were not chosen to succeed Johnson. Almost overnight, security became an issue before Jankovich announced his choice for the new coach. "I had death threats and had to have bodyguards outside my home and outside my office," Jankovich said. "It was not a good situation."

Concerned by the rage, Jankovich met with Foote and Jim McLemore, chairman of the board of regents. "Look, this school is bigger than I am and I know you're going to buy whoever I hire," Jankovich told them. "If this is really going to hurt the university, even though I don't think it's the right decision, you can hire Gary Stevens and I'll try to live with it the best I can."

Jankovich received the university's full support to hire Dennis Erickson. Through Foote, they said they had hired him to make these decisions and they would back him, regardless of who he hired.

Few people in South Florida, including coaches like Tommy Tuberville, had any idea about the spread. They knew football to be a game played with two backs—one primarily a blocker—a tight end, and two wide receivers. The better and faster the receivers, the more likely a defense would have to double cover one of them for safety's sake, thereby leaving the other in one-on-one coverage.

At Miami, they held defenses in place after the snap with play action, just like in the NFL, and then the quarterback would look downfield for a single-covered receiver. When they recruited, Miami coaches would tell players to watch NFL games and pay attention to the offensive style because it was the same offense they used in Coral Gables.

When Erickson and his coaches arrived for a news conference in Miami, they showed up in tweed sport coats that probably made sense in Pullman but made them look like northern tourists in South Florida. Players initially kept their distance, unsure about this new group of coaches, and the talk about changing the offense wasn't limited to the returning players and the media.

"I questioned it," Tuberville said, "but not out loud to [Erickson]. I was thinking, you know, we have a pretty good offense here, we had a quarterback [Steve Walsh] who finished pretty high nationally, and we hadn't had a lot of problems scoring points, so absolutely, yes, I was skeptical."

Tuberville didn't realize that, while Walsh finished sixth nationally in passing, surrounded by the kind of talent most coaches would break rules to get, the national leader in passing the previous season was Washington State's Timm Rosenbach, with nothing close to the cast of characters surrounding him that Walsh enjoyed. Neither did he realize how much Erickson liked to run out of the spread.

"I kept my mouth shut," Tuberville said about the new offense. "Then the first day of [spring] practice, when I saw it and realized what it meant to the defense, I went, 'okay, I get it.'"

The first day of spring practice at the University of Miami in 1989 was unlike anything Dennis Erickson had ever known in football as a player, assistant, or head coach. The level of effort and energy the Hurricanes brought to the field was an immediate, transformational experience.

"Those players educated me, taught me more than I could ever have imagined," Erickson said.

> We practiced hard in high school, or we thought we practiced hard, and when I started coaching I always tried to get the intensity level up so you can really see the outside edge of what people can do, you have to push yourself to get there, a coach yelling at you isn't going to do it.

Wherever I had been, I always thought I was missing something in my coaching because I could never get that sustained intensity from drill to drill, from one day to the next, but the first day I was there I saw those people practice harder than any football team I had ever seen.

I owe those players a debt I could never repay them for opening my eyes to what a real football practice feels like. I can get more out of guys, having been there, but to practice at the level they practiced? That comes from inside, not from some coach telling you to work harder. Those guys brought that with them to practice, it was what they knew, and it was an incredible thing to see.

In his first year at Miami, Erickson did something neither Schnellenberger nor Johnson had accomplished that early—he won a national championship. Miami's Sugar Bowl win over Alabama to wrap up the '89 season confirmed what many had conceded before the game was played. The Hurricanes were clearly the team of the decade when they took home their third national championship since 1983, won under three different coaches. All corners of the media opined on what it meant about the direction of college football, most analysts fretting over possibilities of copycatting the team's intemperate behavior.

Amid the cultural hand-wringing over these outliers from South Beach, large chunks of actual football significance were absent from the analysis. Miami's successes were covered mostly as an unruly insurrection that took over the governor's mansion of the game. Virtually nothing was said about the architecture that drove Miami's offense and the insightful approach of the coach who brought it there, because of the outward appearance of the roster. The substance of what was changing college football and arresting the attention of coaches and players from coast to coast who saw the spread in action was all but lost in the ruckus being raised about these players, their attitudes, and their demeanor.

Legendary *Miami Herald* columnist Edwin Pope was one of the few who saw something original and exceptional in Erickson. He saw it on game days. "There were so many great players on those teams—not just Dennis's, but all three [coaches']—that I got caught up in the overwhelming talent they had," Pope said.

> We had seen two other coaches win in recent years and we all knew this was the new team and we probably didn't spend too much time on the design of the thing; we were caught up in the results.
>
> Looking back on it, the greatest football coach I ever watched over a period of time was [Dolphins coach Don] Shula. If you add everything together, the winning, the discipline, the consistency, toughness, all those things, I don't think there was anyone better than Shula. But I don't believe Dennis ever got the credit he deserved. After all, he won more games than Jimmy or Howard; nobody ever had a winning percentage like Dennis. It didn't help him that there were all those controversies going on around the program, but I think now, and I thought then, of all the coaches I've covered, I never saw one better than Dennis on game day; nobody else had the knack he had to make that perfect call at just the right time.

Erickson's coaches and his players always talk about it, but Pope was one of the few in the media who picked up on it, though there were reasons for the dereliction of journalistic duty. Because it was Miami, the significance of the spread was obscured by a tangle of more readily available issues, such as the team's conduct on and off the field, an emerging team scandal that involved fraudulent Pell Grant applications, the disconnect between university administration and the football team, and more. In Miami there's always something else requiring immediate attention, whether it's the pro sports franchises in town, the alarming gap between rich and poor, the seething cauldron of political unrest associated with various groups of immigrants, or the ever-present celebrities and assorted other beautiful people frolicking at South Beach.

The cultural changes this new crew of athletes brought with them to the UM turned out to be way more interesting to most observers than the structural change in college football that was being made by the spread offense. The emerging philosophy that would reshape the way coaches and recruiters thought about how to play football and what kind of people you needed to play it well wound up lost in the detritus of what Miami presented in the 1980s. In fairness, the talent on defense was such a blinding light that few in the media paused long enough to grasp the significance of a spread offense having just won a national championship for the first time in the history of the game.

A complicating factor for the media emerged soon after Erickson and staff arrived. The local press realized that coaching stories weren't going to be the low-hanging fruit they had been with Johnson, the voluble talker, or with Schnellenberger and his rich history, melded between Bear Bryant and the Dolphins. Schnellenberger knew as well as anyone in coaching that it was part of his job to keep the Hurricanes in the headlines.

With Erickson, South Florida media outlets were confronted with a coach who had no adjacent back story, no storied southern football pedigree, not a hint of twang in his voice like Johnson, no rumbling megaphone of lore such as Schnellenberger represented. Erickson's history was obscure, another son of a high school coach who learned the game from the inside out in a part of the country about as far away from Coral Gables as you could get and still be in the continental United States.

The only aspect of the job Erickson shared with Johnson was the administration's desire to keep Miami football winning and playing in big games on national television. Johnson grew up in a defensive environment and believed in the muscular, pro-style offense; Erickson was a high school and college quarterback who learned to coach running backs, wide receivers, and quarterbacks in college before he became an offensive coordinator. Johnson's offensive approach had an undeniable appeal because it served as a virtual resume for professional scouts to observe. The structure, featuring two hard-running backs in a play-action design, could have been mistaken as having been purloined from a National Football League playbook. Erickson's offense, while unconventional for the time, gave receivers, backs, and quarterbacks even more frequent opportunities to make plays in one-on-one situations all over the field, an undeniable selling point that caused players to eagerly jump on the bus the new coach was driving.

Schnellenberger didn't have to carry the burden of public approval on his shoulders. Quite the contrary, nobody was saying anything about Miami football when he arrived, so any attention he generated was greatly appreciated by the administration. The truth of it is, whether in Coral Gables, Florida, or Manhattan, Kansas, there is always more freedom to pursue winning at a school that has no history than in a place with a tradition and a particular approach to winning such as Penn State, Michigan, Alabama, Oklahoma, or other traditional national powers.

Institutions have personalities just like people and once major college football powers establish theirs, departures from the norm are not well received. Schnellenberger found that out in 1995 when he went to Oklahoma, produced a 5-5-

1 record, and was gone the next year. It wasn't so much the record — Gary Gibbs had been 6-6 the year before Schnellenberger got there — it was the approach, the Schnellenberger package, that didn't impress Sooner Nation. Oklahoma was used to winning the Barry Switzer way, with a triple-option offense that was bursting with speed all over the field, on both sides of the ball. It surprised nobody who knew him that Schnellenberger was going to try to win his way, but it surprised the coach when Oklahomans said, in effect, "Thanks, but no thanks." They knew what they wanted at Oklahoma and he wasn't it.

At Miami they were practically digging the grave for the football program when Schnellenberger arrived, and his style was quickly associated with newfound, big-time success. When Johnson followed that up with his cast of Joe College outcasts, the fan base loved it, even while the administration eventually became appalled. This was the essential point overlooked by the NCAA-centrics who sought to preserve some kind of unwritten rules of college football etiquette. They were in a tizzy over the ways in which the Hurricanes didn't bother staying within the lines of the NCAA coloring book at the same time that they reveled in stories about the grand traditions at Penn State, Oklahoma, or Michigan.

Institutions all grow into their own cultural communities, from the coeds in summer dresses at the University of Mississippi's Grove to the students at Virginia who wear traditional neckties to games on Saturday afternoons to the fans at Washington who arrive by boat after a few Bloody Marys and a lakeside brunch. Miami had started its own tradition when it began heavily recruiting area talent. The fact that a significant percentage of them came from disadvantaged backgrounds that they represented on the football field was no more unusual than the tough country boy approach Bear Bryant built at Alabama.

The necessary ingredients were all in place at Miami. This coach with that offensive design at this particular school with all the talent on hand when Erickson arrived should have been the subject of an ongoing national conversation about the spread. It would have been just that had it not been for the thick stew of cultural conflicts the roster created. It all goes back to Schnellenberger and the impact of his State of Miami recruiting vision.

Schnellenberger saw talent and soon everyone in the eastern half of the United States, and especially the big schools in Florida, would be in to recruit it. The State of Miami, in effect, strengthened four more Division I-A football programs in the state. Because of that rich and previously ignored base of talent, football programs were started at Florida International, Florida Atlantic, and South Florida, and the campus at Central Florida was reinvigorated by the intent to mine riches out of the State of Miami recruiting fields. At the time Schnellenberger didn't understand the impact that talent would have on the university administration and the sense of propriety that the State of Miami would forever alter in the NCAA's football universe.

Considering the ramifications of what the UM football program was becoming takes us on a detour from the straight-line development and implementation of the spread, but you can't describe how the names of Erickson and Elway managed to get lost in the national emergence of the offense without considering what happened at Miami when Erickson coached there. Had those players been a part of the program and the recruiting base all along, Miami football would never have been considered for termination back in the 1970s, there would have been no desperate, last-ditch attempt to bring in a coach like Schnellenberger to save the day, no reason to find one like Johnson to replace him on this wild beast, and there surely would not have been someone like Erickson brought in to show the country a more efficient, more appealing way for recruits to play the game. The fact that Miami's administration wanted Erickson to maintain and extend the championship flavor of the program while simultaneously changing the worldview and on-field personalities of the very players who were recruited to the school because of who they were as football players seems, in hindsight, preposterous at best.

The tone-deaf approach taken by Miami's administration was stunning. When Lou Saban and then Schnellenberger began recruiting the available talent in South Florida, they discovered hard-edged inner-city areas such as Overtown—known as Colored Town at the turn of the twentieth century, when it was among the few areas of the city where blacks were allowed to live—and the destitute sugarcane fields to the north, which were teeming with skilled football players. It could not have been a news flash to the administration that these areas existed in such close proximity to campus. These culturally overlooked areas soon populated the roster with extremely talented players who brought an attitude of ambition and aggression to the program from an underclass culture that desperately wanted to break out and achieve. Saban and Schnellenberger invited them in; the University of Miami was the place and football was their career path.

That was never more evident than in January 1989. Jimmy Johnson was plotting his escape to Dallas a few weeks before Erickson was hired, when a black motorcyclist in Overtown was shot in the back and killed by a police officer. This was six days before Miami hosted the classic Super Bowl XXIII in which Joe Montana took San Francisco 92 yards in the final minutes to pull out a victory over Cincinnati. The week before the game, racial tensions in the city were extremely high, but after the Super Bowl circus came to town, the drama of the finish almost served to distract attention from the racial issues banging against polite white culture.

The atmosphere Erickson entered two months later was a vortex of indignation and barely concealed rage within South Florida's black community, which supplied the Miami football program with the heartbeat and ambition the team had lacked prior to the Schnellenberger-Johnson years. The desire to voice frustrations over the environment in which they lived was heard in the ribald music of hip-hop groups like 2 Live Crew and others. The politics of the area were broiling as always, with local black issues backed against those of immigrants, both legal and otherwise, from Cuba and South America. For Erickson, the message from UM administrators on his way in was clear: instruct your team to act at all times like conscientious young gentlemen.

This is the environment to which Jankovich wanted to bring an offense that an offensive coordinator once described as a "fuck you" approach to traditional college football. Are we surprised there were issues?

Despite the essential obligation for someone in a position of authority to at least listen to the issues of Miami's black underclass, the stated mission of school president Foote was to make the private university an institution someone might think of as the Harvard of the South. For all his establishment knowledge, Foote somehow missed the glaring point that Harvard selected its student body from thousands of applicants all over the country and the world, picking and choosing from a variety of cultures those intellectual attributes that fit neatly in Cambridge, Massachusetts. When Miami selected football players from a wider base up the eastern seaboard, it worked to the detriment of the program and very nearly caused it to be disbanded for a lack of success. When it began recruiting South Florida heavily, sprinkling in national recruits to fill holes, the Hurricanes became winners. Now Foote wanted it both ways, apparently either not understanding or not caring about the reality of the South Florida roots that grew the program into a three-time national champion in a decade.

Hal Mumme, Mike Leach, LaVell Edwards, and Bill Walsh all desired speed but the reality of the times was that there were a lot more sure-handed receivers who weren't fast than there were speed burners. The spread's game-long drumbeat of short out patterns that frustrated defenses—or crossing routes over the middle, with backs or receivers catching passes while running at full speed diagonally through the defense—would generally take its toll, and by the second half the defenders who had been covering those patterns the entire game would become susceptible to a deep ball thrown over their heads. Tightly wound routes eventually opened the way for those slower receivers to gain an advantage later in the game.

Leach, a Mormon who attended BYU before transferring to Pepperdine, watched Edwards's teams with great interest, but from a distance, not connected in any formal way to the BYU team, or any other team in college football. Mumme came up through Texas high school football, had a quarterbacks and receivers assistant's job at West Texas State in 1980 and '81, then landed a more substantial role as the offensive coordinator for Coach Bill Yung at the University of Texas–El Paso from 1982 to '85.

In those days game preparation was done on sixteen-millimeter film instead of tape and digital discs. You would get rotations of three previous games for an upcoming opponent, and because of the random nature of scheduling, you might find yourself watching one particular team over and over: this week in a package of film when they played New

Mexico, last week again when they played San Diego State, the week before when they appeared against Colorado State.

Mumme always seemed to be watching film of BYU, no matter who UTEP was playing that week, so he started studying the way Edwards moved the ball down the field. It was like a clever boxer who could jab and move and take a little slice here, another there, and midway through the fourth quarter the other team would be a mess. Mumme would take his son to Provo, Utah, for a BYU football camp in the summer, affording him the opportunity to spend some time in the film room, going over the Cougars' offense.

"He sort of took me under his wing," Mumme said of those early days when he got to know Edwards. "We beat them the last year I was at UTEP and they couldn't believe we all got fired. He was very kind. I ended up going up there in the spring by myself, then again with my son to the camp in the summer."

Maybe Edwards couldn't believe Yung and his staff had been fired, maybe he was just trying to be gracious. In the four years Mumme was on the staff, UTEP was 7-39; they never won more than one conference game in a season and went winless in the Western Athletic Conference in 1983. In three of the four years Mumme was on the Miners' staff, the team lost ten games, including the final season in 1985 when the team was 1-10, its only victory a stunning 23–16 upset of No. 7 BYU.

UTEP won that game with a bizarre 2-9 defense that forced BYU out of its passing offense that had been averaging 507 yards and thirty-two points a game. Quarterback Robbie Bosco was intercepted four times and BYU's twenty-five-game conference winning streak snapped. It was, without question, the biggest moment for Yung and his staff, but it was far short of enough to forestall the firings that took place at the end of the season.

12

Here It Comes, Hidden in Plain Sight (Mid-1990s)

Johnson took most of his Miami assistants with him to the Cowboys, leaving behind local media favorite and offensive coordinator Gary Stevens. The media openly asked for Stevens's appointment as head coach and questioned the need to look anywhere outside of South Florida. To them, reaching to the far northwest corner of the country to fill a coaching vacancy when South Florida was so loaded with talent and had a qualified assistant all ready to go seemed a waste of time and effort.

"I don't think anyone disliked Erickson when he came in," said *Miami Herald* columnist Dan LeBatard, "but everyone liked Stevens, he was the guy, and really, everyone thought it was on obvious choice.

"We didn't know this guy from the Northwest," LeBatard said. "He seemed okay, but he wasn't one of ours, that's fair, and most of us didn't warm up to him all that much."

There were questions about Athletic Director Sam Jankovich and his apparent obsession with hiring a coach who had hardly captured the nation's attention in his work with the 12-10-1 Cougars in the two previous years. Erickson seemed a good coach to the South Florida media, but what could he have known about Miami, and furthermore, what did it say about Jankovich that after six years at the school his best idea for Johnson's replacement was a guy at Washington Freakin' State?

There's a saying in Florida that geography is reversed, that the most southern part of the state is up north, from Tallahassee on the west to Jacksonville on the east, and the farther south you go, the less it feels southern. By that theory, when you get to Miami, you're in another world, but the South Florida media was playing it old school when it came to finding a new coach.

Tommy Tuberville had his own questions. A young grad assistant coach left behind when Johnson took the Cowboys job, he was just getting started and now this? He had been filled with enthusiasm and, okay, maybe some naïve level of hope after being a part of the Hurricanes, and what exactly would happen to this newborn career in the hands of a guy from Washington State who couldn't possibly be familiar with the area and the particulars of the program?

Tuberville wondered if Miami, with all its talent and swagger, could ever be the place for a guy who had to have a committee meeting in his own head to decide if he wanted to be there. This was, quite possibly, the best coaching job in college football, the program having burst across the national landscape in the last decade as a two-time national champion that sat on the most lucrative recruiting field in the country, and the guy at Washington State wasn't sure he wanted the job?

Washington State? There might be more difficult places to recruit blue-chip football players, but outside of Manhattan, Kansas, Tuberville would have been hard-pressed to name a more isolated locale than Pullman, Washington. At Miami, it was possible, at least in theory, to recruit a top-ten class of talent on a single tank of gas. At Pullman, you had to get on a plane just to be in the proximity of players at a similar talent level, and then you had to persuade them to leave California for a four-year tour in the remote Eastern Washington farmlands, a place with no chance to win a national championship.

The persistence of Jankovich also kept Tuberville wondering. Twice Erickson had declined Jankovich's offer, but the Miami AD wasn't about to let go. He knew Erickson better than most, having been on Jim Sweeney's staff at Montana State when Erickson enrolled as a freshman quarterback. He knew Erickson was building a winner at Washington State with decidedly less talent and financing than most schools. Because he had background knowledge, Jankovich was absorbed with the thought of what Erickson's offense might be capable of when his talent was superior to that of his opponents.

Jankovich realized Erickson's offense used four receivers and defenses were forced into constant one-on-one coverage, he understood the depth of talent in the Miami program, and he was very aware of how much more talent was out there in South Florida wanting to be part of a national championship Hurricanes football team. That's why he kept calling Erickson back.

At first, Erickson dismissed it out of hand, perceiving it as a flattering gesture from an old friend and colleague. He was a Northwest guy and if Idaho, being a I-AA school, wasn't the ideal location for him, Washington State, just eight miles down the road and over the border, was as close to perfection as he had imagined.

At each step along the way, Erickson's moves were not only a step up in class for him, they also brought better salaries to his coaching staff. This one would mean more money than any of his coaches had ever made. The Miami commitment was to pay the staff at a level in the mix with the best-paid staffs in the country. More money for everyone, yet this was the job offer that had Erickson pacing, stalling, questioning his thoughts and his purpose. He never wanted bigger, he just wanted a chance to win, and he had grown to the precise place he wanted to be. Then he realized something Jankovich said was true: "Dennis, you can win national championships here."

He accepted.

Mike Leach and Hal Mumme caught the bug.

While the spread offense taking over college football was not a topic of conversation in the sports media, it was absolutely on the minds of football coaches, especially young ones like Leach and Mumme looking for way into the profession. First Mumme and then Leach came to be portrayed in the media as offensive innovators, leaning on their creativity and smarts. They have come to represent the outer limits of the spread offense—passing version—staying one step ahead of defensive schemes while trashing the traditional importance of the running game.

Ahead of the curve, they say about these guys, but if they were really free thinkers with insight on tomorrow, they would have had tape recorders with them in the late 1980s and early '90s when they were storming around the country like some Butch Cassidy and Sundance Kid gridiron buddy team, looking for football players and seeking wisdom from successful coaches. Tapes from those stream-of-consciousness conversations on long car rides would be valuable commodities today for Leach, now the Washington State coach, and Mumme, hired in 2013 as associate head coach to June Jones at SMU.

Mumme was at home in Texas, where he got some unconventional ideas about moving the ball offensively. After four years at UTEP, where he was able to drill into the BYU passing offense in the off-season, he coached at Copperas Cove (TX) High School from 1986 to 1989, then left to take his visionary football concepts into a small college setting at Iowa Wesleyan, an NAIA school in Mount Pleasant, a town of eighty-five hundred in the southeastern portion of the state.

Little more than riding shotgun, second in charge on the two-man team at Iowa Wesleyan, was Leach, a guy who played football only sparingly in high school—never as a starter—didn't play at all in college, and after graduating from Pepperdine Law School one day announced to his wife, Sharon, that he'd decided he wanted to be a college football coach. Some of them are saints on firm ground, these women who put up with coaches like Leach. It must be comparable to the experience of being married to a traveling folk singer, only with short-sleeve polyester coaches' shirts, in this case emblazoned with a Tigers logo. That would be the mascot at Iowa Wesleyan.

A disruption in the normal order of things occurred in Mount Pleasant in 1989, the year Erickson went to Miami, when the school hired Mumme to be its football coach. He brought along the defensive coordinator from Copperas Cove and wound up hiring Leach to coach the offense, partly because of Leach's intellect and interest in the passing game and partly because there weren't a lot of other applicants. "I wanted to take my offensive coordinator from Copperas," Mumme said, "but he couldn't afford the pay cut. The OC only paid about $12,000 and you had to do about ten different jobs."

The connective tissue between Mumme and Leach was an interest in the passing game of BYU coach LaVell Edwards, who, along with Bill Walsh—with the Cincinnati Bengals and then later at Stanford and with the San Francisco 49ers—was among the first to begin horizontal exploration of defenses. Edwards and Walsh mostly operated out of two-back formations and wanted to control tempo with short passes, unlike the spread, which did it with one or no backs. It was a brainy approach because, from its start in the late nineteenth century, football had always been a straight-ahead game, with flying wedges in which bruising fullbacks slammed into toothless linebackers to kick open a door for a hunch-shouldered back to gain a few yards.

Walsh first came up with his plan as an assistant coach in Cincinnati for the legendary Paul Brown when they lost a rocket-armed starter named Greg Cook to an injury. His backup was Virgil Carter, whose arm was in a different league from Cook's, but Carter was a brainiac—a statistics student from BYU, of all places—and a player who instantly grasped the wisdom of Walsh's new scheme.

The concept was to use both backs, both receivers, and a tight end as potential pass catchers in a system that relied on a quick rhythm, almost like choreography. All five could be in swirling, slanting pass patterns at the same time, running precision routes, releasing a few steps downfield, then moving out toward the sidelines, forcing defenses to cover the field horizontally. Carter would take a three- to five-step roll and fire a pass in those short zones. They called it dink and dunk, and it was pretty much the same approach Edwards used at BYU with his generally slower groups of receivers, who also used tight, precise routes to their advantage. Unlike the run-and-shoot, which required two slotbacks—basically the old Dutch Meyer double wing from TCU—the packages Edwards and Walsh formulated were heavy on bang-bang timing and crossing routes, always with the threat of a run or a quick pass to a back when the linebackers would begin to pinch in too close.

Mumme and Leach liked the general idea, but they weren't interested in copying anybody. They wanted to personalize and expand the concept. Not so much running is what they came up with. Moving the ball, gaining first downs was the idea, and if they could do it all day by passing, who needed to run?

By the time Miami opened the 1989 season, high schools in Florida, California, Oregon, Washington, and Texas were using the spread offense because it was so simple to teach and players were able to practice it all summer long. The months between spring football and fall camp became a time of productive growth for quarterbacks, receivers, and running backs whose coaches were installing the spread. Mike Price used to call it "legalized cheating" because his quarterbacks and receivers liked nothing more than tossing the ball around over the summer and every time they did it, it improved their timing and polished their skills.

Meanwhile, the Hurricanes pushed and challenged each other on a daily basis in ways that made their coaches gush with pride. It would be one player yelling at another, demanding more, each one trying to exceed the other in terms of energy expended.

They would fight, literally, swinging fists on the practice field, then after practice the same players could be seen walking arm-in-arm to the showers. It was a war zone on those practice fields every day, a legacy from some of the hard neighborhoods they had survived growing up, from the brutal demands of Schnellenberger years earlier, and maybe more than any other factor, it was a response to what Erickson called the X factor at Miami.

"It wasn't us, it wasn't the coaches," Erickson said. "Nobody understands the bond those kids had playing at that school. The ones who were there before them? Michael Irvin, Randy Shannon, Bennie Blades, all of them were in constant contact with those players who followed them. They were on the phone with them all the time, they'd come by in spring and challenge them in workouts, they talk about the tradition, about championships, about the U, I'm telling you, it's an incredible thing.

"All the psychology that goes into football, the mental edge and how to maintain it?" Erickson said. "As coaches at Miami after a while, we realized we didn't even have to get involved with that, all the ex-players were doing that for us, getting them at a competitive edge, so we just had to concern ourselves with game plans and stuff. Those guys were ready for anything we threw at them.

"It was," he said, "the greatest experience I've ever had as a head coach."

Erickson's run at Miami was more successful than any coach's in school history and one of the best of all time in college football over a six-year span. His Miami teams were 63-9, an .875 winning percentage that exceeded Jimmy Johnson's, Howard Schnellenberger's, and all the others'. In six years Erickson's team won two national championships and played for two others. He was the first coach since Michigan's Bennie Oosterbaan in 1948 to win a national championship in his first season with a team.

His critics in South Florida, the Gary Stevens faction, discounted his first championship because they said he was winning with Johnson's players, but Johnson had success with Schnellenberger's players, and after Erickson left, players he recruited stuffed the top of the NFL draft. He clearly benefited from the Miami tradition, and the tradition benefited from him.

Tuberville's initial concerns were mitigated by the fact that Erickson told him he didn't want to change a thing about the 4-3 defense that was among the best in the country, probably the best in the decade of the 1980s, at the least. Erickson showed his staff and the players he knew something about defense, too, after he demoted starting defensive tackle Jimmy Jones and replaced him with a young player named Cortez Kennedy, who had come from a junior college in Arkansas. When he got there, Erickson told Kennedy he had great talent but he lacked the personal motivation required to raise his level of effort in practice to where it needed to be to compete for a starting position.

"[Erickson] told me if I outworked guys it wouldn't go unnoticed, and he said my effort in practice was going to determine if I ever got on the field," Kennedy said. "I looked up to Jimmy Jones, but I wanted to play, too, so I took him at his word and worked to get that job."

Kennedy got the message, cranked up the intensity in practice, won the job, and was paired inside the Miami defensive line with Russell Maryland to form perhaps as imposing a set of defensive tackles as has ever played together in college football. Kennedy entered the Pro Football Hall of Fame in 2012.

There is some truth to the observation made after the 1989 season that, given the strength of the defense, it wouldn't have mattered what kind of offense the Hurricanes employed. Miami went ten quarters at one point in the season without allowing a touchdown and it surrendered an average of just 9.3 points per game all season. Quarterback Craig Erickson, no relation to the new coach, was surrounded by a tremendous array of talent that allowed him to ease into his role in the new offense. They opened with a 51–3 win at Wisconsin and backed it up with a 31–3 rout of California the next week and a 38–7 win at Missouri.

That made it a combined 120–13 in the first three weeks and it looked like nothing had changed, which was part of the problem. The taunting didn't cease, and after watching one of his players perform a little dance step after hitting a Missouri player so hard he lay motionless on the field, Erickson spoke out about it, saying, "I never liked taunting, I never will, and I'm going to do whatever I can to eliminate what could even appear to be taunting."

The players were on better behavior the rest of the season, losing only to Florida State at Tallahassee when the quarterback Erickson missed the game with an injury and inexperienced backup Gino Torretta—intercepted four times—wasn't up to the task, which seemed to affect the rest of the team. Miami was stopped on three different occasions at the Florida State 1-yard line. They came back strong, winning the next three games by a combined 108–19 to set up a home game against Notre Dame that could lift them into a national championship opportunity.

The November 25 meeting in the Orange Bowl was another of the grudge matches between the schools that had been spiced with trash talking, scuffles, and generally bad behavior on both sides when the rival coaches were Lou Holtz and Jimmy Johnson. This time, a memorable twenty-two-play drive was the catalyst that gave Miami a 27–10 victory and an invitation to play Alabama in the Sugar Bowl.

Less than a year after taking the Cougars to a bowl game in Hawaii, a remarkable achievement for Washington State, Erickson was coaching against Alabama for a national championship. A long, strange trip from Pullman, indeed.

When they got to New Orleans, it was as though they were hustled in and out of public view through the stage-door entrance. Alabama was the object of attention for the news media and the Sugar Bowl Committee seemed to defer to the desires of the Crimson Tide while expecting the Hurricanes to go along with whatever role they were offered in the festivities leading up to the game. All of that was fine with Erickson, who couldn't help but think back to the time Bear Bryant flew to Montana State for the Bobcats' awards banquet following Erickson's senior season. Erickson had won team and conference awards and felt sweat run down his forehead when Bryant called his name, turned on stage, and held a hand out to shake. "All I remember is that my hand was dripping sweat and I was scared to death," Erickson said. "Shaking his hand wasn't something I ever figured was going to happen."

In the lead-up to the Sugar Bowl, the extra attention being afforded to Alabama went over less well with the Miami players, who felt they were being slighted. That sentiment was fine with Erickson. Being a first-year coach, he was happy to lay back in the weeds and let most of the attention go to Alabama coach Bill Curry, who had been voted the Bobby Dodd Coach of the Year a week before the game, despite an undercurrent of discontent from Tide fans. It was Curry's third season in Tuscaloosa and he had never been a fan favorite, for one, because he was a Georgia Tech graduate, and for another, because everyone had assumed that when Ray Perkins left Alabama to coach Tampa Bay of the NFL, the job was going to go to Florida State's Bobby Bowden.

"It was the only job I really went after," Bowden said of his Hall of Fame career that included thirty-three years at Florida State. "I thought that might be a place we could do well and sure, I thought I might get it, but Bill Curry got the last interview and whatever he said must have been what they wanted to hear."

Curry's best season at Alabama was 1989, but he made the mistake of losing to Auburn all three seasons, and the '89 loss was more galling than any of them to Tide fans because it was the first game ever played in Auburn. The game had always been staged at Legion Field in Birmingham, 58 miles from Tuscaloosa, 110 miles from Auburn. The rationale was that the stadium in Birmingham was larger than the facilities at either Auburn or Tuscaloosa, allowing more fans to attend the game. When Auburn's Jordan-Hare Stadium was expanded to fit more fans than Legion Field, a new deal was brokered and the Tigers got to play their most bitter enemies at home every other season.

When Alabama lost that first game at Auburn, Curry knew he was in trouble. The fan base was on edge, school president Joab Thomas was forced out in 1988, and Director of Athletics Steve Sloan, who played quarterback for Bryant after Joe Namath moved on to professional football, was out after 1989.

Miami won the Sugar Bowl, 33–25, but the score was deceiving in that the Hurricanes had the game well in command before Alabama scored in the fourth quarter to make the final result appear closer than the game itself.

At the end of the game, Curry called his coaching staff together in a small room that adjoined the Crimson Tide locker room in the bowels of the Superdome. "It was a big secret," recalled Tommy Bowden, Bobby's son and, at the time, Curry's wide receivers coach. "He said he was going up to Kentucky to talk to them about a job, but he didn't want anybody to know; he was telling us so we wouldn't be surprised but he didn't want it leaking out, he wanted us all to keep quiet."

That was almost as hard to do then as it is today. Bowden remembered walking out of the Superdome and across the plaza to the Hyatt Regency Hotel next door. He took the elevator up to his room, inserted the key, opened the door, and saw his wife, Linda, sitting on the edge of the bed, television off, the room quiet. She had a familiar look on her face.

"We're moving again, aren't we?" she said.

Not long after Erickson used the spread successfully at Washington State, it started leaving marks everywhere.

That process began when Baylor was ambushed at home

by San Jose State in 1980 and high school and college coaches in Texas started inquiring about those game tapes. What had that West Coast team done to Baylor's defense? Were the Bears looking past them?

Stanford used the spread starting in 1984, when Jack Elway took over as coach and managed a few upsets of his own, including a big one over Texas in 1987. By that time several coaches in the Southwest had disregarded or already forgotten the impact of San Jose State's undressing of Baylor in 1980.

"I remember in 1987 I was at Texas A&M when TCU was a split-back veer team," said Bob Davie, who went on to coach at Notre Dame from 1997 to 2001, "and we ran the same strong safety blitz twenty-five times in one game, the same exact blitz. It was so much easier to play defense; the advantage of it was that you spent so much more time on technique, you didn't have to spend really any time at all on recognition and getting lined up."

The spread forced defensive coaches to completely alter their philosophies and coaching styles, not because they wanted to, because they had to. "On defense, I used to say, 'Get your cleats in the ground and get set to play,'" said Davie.

The way football is now, because of the spread, there's no question it's a matter of spreading people out and not letting them get their cleats in the ground and get set. Our kids knew exactly what was coming that time against TCU, they knew the defense, so you just called it, repeatedly. Defense is recognition of seeing the same things over and over so you can worry about what you're going to do, not what the offense is going to do. This thing has now become totally reactive, where the defense is waiting to see what the offense is going to do and then you're reacting, you don't get settled in and ready like you used to be able to do.

In a nutshell, Davie, a defensive specialist, described the intended purpose of the spread, namely to get defenses out of position and clueless about what's coming next. In the spread you can run or pass from any formation and the presnap motion can absolutely disguise what's coming next.

"There used to be a thing you called gang tackling, where you could have seven, eight, or nine guys swarming to the ball and as coaches you would grade your tape based on gang tackles: how many guys did we get around the ball?" Davie said. "Well, the spread has almost eliminated that, it's all one-on-one tackling all over the field because you're so far from your teammates—the offense is spread, that makes you spread—there's no huddling, there's no gang tackling. The personnel you play on defense these days has changed, everything about defense has changed in a dramatic, top-to-bottom way because of the spread."

Steele got an up-close look at the point of the spear in the coming change when Washington State came to Knoxville in 1988, while Steele was on the coaching staff of Johnny Majors. "[Defensive coordinator] Ken Donahue was a tremendous football coach, really a legend of sorts in the South as far as great coordinators go; the man had six national championship rings and the respect of everyone who was ever around him," Steele said. "But we all had trouble that day against Washington State. It's hard to put it out of your mind. As far as I know, that was the first time a team from out west came into the South and really just put on a clinic on where football was headed. To me, that season, with [offensive coordinator Walt] Harris putting our offense into motion and us guys on defense having to readjust to it, and then that Washington State game—that's when I would say college football started changing because of the spread, 1988, or the late '80s in general."

Donahue played for Tennessee on its 1951 national championship team and coached for Bryant with five Alabama champions. He is considered an innovator of multiple defenses for the way he was able to instruct techniques that allowed players to shift from a 4-3 front to a 5-2 defense without losing continuity.

For all his experience and ability, Donahue had never seen anything like what he faced that night against Washington State quarterback Timm Rosenbach, receiver Tim Stallworth, and running back Steve Broussard. The spread offense put the Tennessee defense in a place it had never been, in its own stadium.

Donahue's plan was to "spot drop" his linebackers into pass coverage. An inside linebacker would drop to a spot on the field about 10–12 yards from the line of scrimmage, 2 yards inside the hash mark. The outside linebacker would drop to a similar spot, closer to the sideline, then they would each break up on the ball when a pass was thrown in their area.

"Washington State had these receivers coming off the line of scrimmage untouched, running underneath routes and seam routes and they're getting the ball in a hurry," Steele said.

I mean, the quarterback was taking three quick steps and the ball was out so you could forget about doing anything with your pass rush, all that did was open the field up a little more for him; our guys were spread out all across the field and we had a linebacker, probably about six foot three, 225 pounds who ran a 4.8 40 who could stuff a run up the middle in his sleep, and he's now out there trying to get to his spot when these guys are catching the ball at full speed in front of him and working their way into those huge seams because we were spread so far apart.

At times it was a wonder that we ever even got a hand on them, the way they were going.

In 1988 Tennessee had a defensive package that included both 4-3 and 5-2 fronts, but neither of those schemes offered any help for an empty backfield, a superior receiver like Steve Broussard at the running back position going in motion, and four other wideouts. Donahue resigned after that game, the last he ever coached. Steele was reassigned and took on additional duties, then left for a linebacker job the following season on the staff of Tom Osborne at Nebraska, where they were still playing three-back football in the Big 8 Conference.

Nebraska was caught flush in the middle of the transition in college football. From 1987 to 1993, when the spread offense was beginning to filter into the bloodstream of the game, Nebraska was 43-5-1 in the Big 8 Conference, but it lost seven consecutive bowl games, including four to Florida State and two to Miami. The Cornhuskers were dominating the run-oriented conference they were in while teams beginning to use spread concepts were drilling them.

It all came to a head in 1991 when Nebraska opened with victories over Utah State (59–28) and Colorado State (71–14), rolling up a margin of 130–35 before its third game of the season, when Washington came to visit Lincoln.

The Huskies, coached by Don James, had owned the Northwest for much of his reign but had lost to Erickson's Cougars, 32–21, in the cross-state rivalry game in 1988 that sent Washington State to the Aloha Bowl and knocked the Huskies out of bowl consideration. When Erickson went to Miami the following year, James hired Keith Gilbertson, Erickson's offensive coordinator, to be his line coach in Seattle as an assistant to offensive coordinator Gary Pinkel. "Do I remember?" said Pinkel of the transition Washington made to the spread offense that had introduced by its in-state rival. "You're talking about the time Nick Saban cost me a national championship."

Pinkel was having fun with a long-running joke between himself and his friend Saban. In 1991 Pinkel had left Washington to be the head coach at Toledo, following his former Kent State teammate Saban, who had coached there for only one year. Saban had lobbied to get Pinkel the job. The next season the 1992 Huskies shared a memorable national championship that would have irrevocably stamped the spread as the game-changing offense of the era had anyone been paying attention. Instead, most reporters were caught up in the personalities and missed the underlying point.

At that 1991 Nebraska-Washington game, trying to outmatch the Washington spread on the Nebraska sideline was Steele, who later coached in the NFL as an assistant with the Carolina Panthers, had an ill-fated stint as head coach at Baylor, and then became one of the college game's most high-profile defensive coordinators at Florida State, Alabama, and Clemson. He saw the spread change football from Lincoln, Nebraska, where running was the offensive key to victory.

"We had a look at it that time in Tennessee but I went to Nebraska. Out there, in that conference, nobody was spreading the field, you know?" he said. "It was 1991 when we had our eyes opened by Washington; they came in and went up and down the field on us. I think we had the lead early but they got it going and we couldn't stop them."

Nebraska was up 21–10 midway through the third quarter when Washington had a touchdown pass by Billy Joe Hobert called back on a holding penalty. Hobert then scrambled up the middle for a 19-yard gain, but it was fourth and eight at the Cornhuskers' 30 when James had trouble with his headset up to the box where Gilbertson, the offensive coordinator, was calling plays.

"I was trying to talk to Gilby and the connection was down or something," James said. "We had a good drive going and I didn't want to try a long field goal, so I said, 'Fuck it, let's go for it.'"

Hobert hit Orlando McKay for a 15-yard gain and a first down at the 15. On the next play, Beno Bryant burst up the middle for a touchdown to make it 21–16 at the end of the quarter. Then Washington scored again, and again, and again in a 36–21 win that sparked a level of confidence that carried the Huskies to an undefeated season.

At the end, Washington crushed Oregon State (58–6) and Washington State (56–21) before beating Michigan 34–14 in the Rose Bowl to earn a share of the national championship with Miami, which won its piece of the title—its second in three years for Erickson—with a 22–0 victory over that same Nebraska squad in the Orange Bowl.

The Cornhuskers had lost to the two teams that shared the national championship, each of them using the spread offense, by a combined score of 58–21. In its other ten games, Nebraska outscored the opposition 433–172, an average of 43–17 per game. Something needed to change in Lincoln.

The spread offense won its first national title in 1989 at Miami, and in 1991 it won two national championships at opposite ends of the country in the same season, with Erickson's former offensive coordinator at Washington State implementing the system at cross-state rival Washington. Erickson had his fingerprints all over it, but the media failed to pick up on the trend.

Again, coaches noticed. The spread started popping up all over and how to defend it became a top priority.

"That was the first time in my career that we really began developing personnel packages to address the spread offenses," Steele said of the 1991 Nebraska season.

That offseason was totally dedicated to going out west, to getting with some teams to figure out what they were doing because they all had a bunch of different defensive packages.

Conceptually, from a defensive standpoint, what you hear in NFL meeting rooms or in a Nick Saban meeting room is, "How can we affect the quarterback?" If you can't do it with the pass rush because the ball is out too quick, the only thing you can do is make it so he doesn't know what he's looking at; he thinks he's seeing this coverage, but he's really seeing *that* coverage, so you have to build these personnel groupings that says, "When they're in this four receiver package, we go to this," or whatever it might be.

These days, defense is nothing like it used to be, because of the spread. It's all philosophically based as opposed to tactically based, the way it used to be. Now you have a library of personnel packages you have on your shelf that you use in these different combinations. It's the whole range of things you have to do to play basketball on grass, that's what it comes down to.

Still valid, that many years later, the concept that occurred to Jack Neumeier when he sat in the stands of a high school basketball game in 1970. The pass went from the wing to the post and, in not so many words perhaps, something clicked in Neumeier. *Basketball on grass.*

"All of a sudden," Steele said,

we have catch zone and man zone, concepts you never heard before the spread. Catch zone is a term for, rather than coming up to the line and pressing the receiver, you play off the line like you're in zone, but you're really in man coverage; I come off at the snap backpedaling like I'm in zone, then I set up and catch the receiver in a man-on-man defense. The receiver is trained to think, "If he's in a zone, I convert my route to this pattern," so you try to make him think that's what you're doing by the way you start off, so he thinks the wrong thing.

In match zone you drop to a certain spot and as the receivers unfold in their routes, you match up, like in basketball, and pick up your man. We used to drop to a spot and try to pick somebody up with linebackers, but now we might be doing it with six defensive backs, and we might be in catch man on one side of the field [and] match man on the other side; anything you can do to confuse the quarterback.

When football started, defense was a lot more manageable. Offenses knew their place: they wanted to run the ball and eat up the clock, shorten the game, and turn it over to their defense, which would usually face the same approach from the opponent's offense.

"It's much more complex than it used to be, because of the spread, but it's the only thing you can do," Steele said. "They forced us into this and I don't think you'll ever see us go back to what it used to be. The money people pay for their seats these days? Now you're going to charge them that much to see the fullback run off tackle?

"I don't think so."

13

Here, There, Everywhere
(Late 1990s, Early 2000s)

Hal Mumme had become a frequent guest of the BYU staff those three years he coached at Copperas Cove and he continued to come back after he was hired at Iowa Wesleyan. As with all NAIA schools, Iowa Wesleyan offered no athletic scholarships. As such, there were fewer restrictions on coaches contacting players, which Mumme interpreted as an open invitation to drive around, talk to coaches on other teams, and meet players and try to sell them on his new offense.

"We were allowed to recruit constantly," Mumme said, "so we'd go see people anywhere we could. We basically would go anywhere we heard somebody was good at throwing the ball and had an idea that we liked. We studied a lot, we drove all over, looking for players, talking to people about the passing game; we got a lot accomplished on those trips, we learned a ton."

At the time Mumme and Mike Leach were formulating the structure of what they would later call the air raid offense. Just a push of a button on an old tape recorder would have done the trick. How much would those road tapes be worth these days?

"We had no money to start with, none," Mumme said. "We were spending out of our own pockets on those deals, going wherever we could that we thought we could find a player or pick up an idea. I mean, it was great in a way, not that I'd want to do it again, but we were younger, we were getting started, and we were sort of on a mission.

"We didn't adapt everything we heard. Some of it was sort of confirming what we were already thinking," he said, "and some of it was pretty technical coaching stuff. Like, once we went to Miami to see what Dennis Erickson was doing and he had this deal about vertical routes, the specific techniques he used for the receivers and how to get over the top of the defensive backs, 'highpointing' the catch—it's something we still use today. There was a lot of stuff like that, a small technical point that, at the time, you couldn't say, 'Man, that made it worth the trip,' but looking back, all that stuff helped us put things together."

In his first year at Iowa Wesleyan, Mumme installed his passing offense with the leftover talent, which wasn't a lot. He remembers a 47–46 loss to Greenville College, a small, Christian liberal arts school outside of St. Louis that had beaten Iowa Wesleyan 52–0 the previous year. "We lost the game, but they never stopped us," Mumme said, "and at that point I think we realized we had some players that were going to be successful there and that our style of play was one of the reasons."

Mumme would take anyone eligible to play who could catch or pass. Smaller guys had a place there. Guys like Dana Holgorsen, a small but tough receiver who had no other offers, enrolled and learned the embryonic stages of the air raid offense. Holgorsen didn't become a great college football player, but he is becoming a highly successful coach at West Virginia, using the Leach-Mumme passing-game principles.

In his second year at Iowa Wesleyan, Mumme met Tony Franklin, a high school coach from Kentucky who was coaching a run-and-shoot offense. Franklin was looking for a place a couple of his receivers might have a chance to play college football.

"I had a couple kids who could catch the ball but had no speed," Franklin said. "I called a buddy of mine in Texas, who said, 'Call this guy named Hal Mumme at Iowa Wesleyan, he'll take anybody.' I'd never heard of him but I drove those kids out there; they didn't end up going there but I had a quarterback who went there in his third year."

Mumme gradually began to attract better players as his contacts with high school coaches expanded and the opportunities available in his offense for receivers with good hands and quarterbacks who knew how to get rid of the ball became more well known. There were a lot of capable players who didn't get scholarship offers to bigger schools but had some ability and a big desire to compete. At the NAIA level, that was enough to be successful.

Leach, who had moved his family from California for the $12,000-a-year job, was eager to move up in the profession. He had taken a job at the College of the Desert, not far from Palm Springs, California, and worked for a short time with a club team in Finland before hooking up with Mumme. Leach heard about an opening at Valdosta State University and sent them Mumme's resume, which was a good thing because at the end of Mumme's third year and a 10-2 season, Iowa Wesleyan was ready for a new coach; Mumme was hired at the Division II school in southern Georgia. In court depositions years later that followed his ouster at Kentucky, Mumme said he was fired at Iowa Wesleyan, but a school administrator made no such claim, while allowing that there was serious administrative concern about Mumme and his spending habits.

When Mumme was hired, Iowa Wesleyan was down to approximately four hundred full-time students and was considering dropping the football program to save money. On a much smaller scale, it was the same sort of discussion they were having in South Florida prior to Schnellenberger's tenure. Mumme was the Howard Schnellenberger of Iowa Wesleyan.

In his first year, Mumme's new team went 7-4 and then backed it up with a 7-5 season in 1990 before the final 10-2 record in 1991 that included a trip to a postseason playoff game in Minnesota that developed into a topic of administrative concern. In three years Mumme was 24-11, still the best stretch of success in school history, but it came with a price.

In his second year he helped arrange an extra game—they called it the Steamboat Classic Bowl—with Olivet Nazarene, a small private school in Illinois. In his third year, when IWC qualified for an NAIA playoff game in Minnesota, Mumme flew the team to the game rather than following standard operating procedure and taking the bus. Iowa Wesleyan lost the game and administrators drew a line in the sand over expenses.

Despite the cost, Mumme's football team helped raise awareness of the school, which today has a student body roughly double the size it was before he arrived.

The two wild and crazy passing offense coaches had immediate success at Valdosta State, resurrecting the program and bringing attention to their approach, really, for the first time. Franklin stayed in touch as he continued to coach his run-and-shoot offense at Calloway County High School, and when support for Kentucky head coach Bill Curry dried up, Franklin was among a group of coaches who successfully lobbied for Mumme. What followed when the school hired Mumme was one of the wildest rides through the SEC that the venerable king of college football conferences had ever seen.

Franklin took it upon himself to organize a group of well-known area high school coaches to encourage Kentucky athletic director C. M. Newton, who built his reputation as a basketball coach, to consider the application and experiences of Mumme before hiring a new football coach. Franklin's efforts paid off.

Newton, originally hired to rebuild a basketball program that had fallen into NCAA probation, pulled off that accomplishment by hiring Rick Pitino, a big-name, high-profile coach who returned the glory of UK basketball almost immediately. Mumme was a different matter, in more ways than one. He was unknown except to college football coaches and insiders, and what he was proposing to put on the field in Lexington was an offense unlike anything that had been seen in the SEC. It wasn't just a departure from tradition, it was a leap of faith into a new world nobody really knew much about.

The Wildcats were 5-6 in 1997, Mumme's first year, boosted by an opening 38–24 win over in-state rival Louisville and the excitement the fan base had for an extreme passing offense that seemed to shake things up in the SEC. They didn't win big, but they did score a lot, taking all kinds of risks as Mumme became known for almost habitually gambling on fourth down, often converting fourth and fifteen or twenty into first downs. That first year, Kentucky was taken apart by Florida, 55–28, but it caused Gators defensive coordinator Bob Stoops to take notice in the sense that only two other teams scored more points on Stoops's defense all season. Mumme had a brilliant young quarterback, Tim Couch, who adapted so well to the offense that he became the No. 1 selection in the NFL draft.

Mumme's base concept was to orchestrate eight to ten pass plays and work them continuously every day in practice on the theory that his team's complete knowledge of those plays would always stand a chance of succeeding because the opponents would practice against it only for the allotted twenty hours of preparation once a year. To the extent that it increased Kentucky's profile, brought a new energy to the football program, and made Tim Couch a well-known quarterback to anyone who followed college football, Mumme's plan succeeded.

It all eventually ran aground in 2001, when assistant coach Claude Bassett, the subject of an NCAA investigation, admitted sending money directly to a high school football coach and improperly allocating money from a Mumme camp. By the time Mumme resigned over recruiting violations, Leach had moved on two years earlier to take the offensive coordinator position at Oklahoma for Bob Stoops, who had accepted his first head-coaching position and wanted the style of offense he had had to defend against when he coached for Steve Spurrier at Florida.

The University of Florida was always one of those schools that had the resources but for one reason or another was never able to get over the top in football, until Steve Spurrier came along. The school's former Heisman Trophy winner and a one-time NFL quarterback, Spurrier brought his pass-oriented offense to the Southeastern Conference at just the right time in the 1990s.

He built an impressive coaching reputation on the strength of his guile and creativity with a passing game that, in its time, was more sophisticated than most college defensive coordinators got to see. Spurrier had a particular, personalized offense that in broad outline mimicked Bill Walsh's West Coast offense, with two running backs who could catch and run and a variety of crossing routes blended in with curls and deep outs. Spurrier kept everyone guessing and turned Southeastern Conference defenses inside out.

"Back then we would fling it around pretty good, it kept those other guys off balance a little bit," Spurrier said. "But you needed to be able to run the ball, too, and we were able to that, thanks, probably, to the way we passed it around."

These days the Walsh offense, or close facsimiles of it, are pretty much seen only in the NFL, where coaches routinely put in seventh to eighty hours a week on game plans and practices and players have the time required to sift through the many details of the scheme, both on the field and in meeting rooms. College coaches can work as much as they want each week, but players are available to them for only twenty hours, which as much as anything explains why the full expression of Walsh's West Coast offense is found only in the pro game. But even so, with Walsh, Spurrier, and Erickson, the running game was always important.

Not everyone realized, because of the vertiginous array of his receivers' routes and the deceptive window dressing Spurrier concocted in the passing game, that it was his running game that made the offense click. Stuff the run and you had something close to a fifty-fifty shot at defending the passing game. It didn't make for great odds, but if you had corners who could cover and a smart safety who could run, your defense had hope if the guys up front could shut the door on the run. On the other hand, if you couldn't shut down Spurrier's running game, you weren't going to beat Florida.

He won three SEC championships—two against Alabama—but couldn't get his alma mater a national championship, even as his reputation as a master at the passing game grew annually. Spurrier's decision to hire a top defensive assistant finally helped get the job done and brought Florida its first national championship at the end of the 1996 season. Spurrier hired Bob Stoops off the staff of Bill Snyder at Kansas State University prior to that season. The previous year Florida had risen to No. 2 nationally in the polls after it won the Southeastern Conference championship with its first undefeated season and landed a spot in the Fiesta Bowl, where it was poised to meet No. 1 Nebraska for a championship. Instead, Florida was denied again after the Gators were humiliated in a 62–24 defeat.

Nebraska stuffed the Gators' run and then some. The Cornhuskers held Florida to minus-28 yards on twenty-one rushing attempts, but much of that was confused by the way they collect statistics in college football, with yards lost in passing—quarterback Danny Wuerffel had lost 37 yards on seven sacks—figured into the rushing totals. There was no question that Spurrier was disgusted by his team's inability to run the ball, but more than that, Florida allowed a bowl-record 524 rushing yards by Nebraska, including 199 by quarterback Tommie Frazier and 165 more by running back Lawrence Phillips. It was a complete breakdown, but Spurrier looked at the scoreboard and thought, even with a bad day offensively, twenty-four points shouldn't leave you more than five touchdowns behind. That game ended up being the moment that connected Steve Spurrier with Bob Stoops and later brought Florida a national championship.

After the humiliating loss to Nebraska, defensive coordinator Bob Pruett, who previously had visions of becoming the Gators' head coach, was hired as the head coach at Marshall University after Jim Donnan accepted the vacant job at Georgia. Spurrier wanted a new, younger coach and he found the right guy when he hired Stoops. The year before, as co-defensive coordinator with Jim Leavitt at Kansas State, Stoops was part of a staff that finished the season with the nation's No. 1–ranked defense in a conference in which Nebraska led the nation in scoring.

Stoops knew what it took to stop a team like Nebraska and Spurrier respected that. In his first year with Spurrier, Florida won the national title in a 52–20 rout of Florida State. In three seasons in Gainesville, Stoops was part of Gators teams that went 31-5. When Oklahoma called, offering Stoops a head coaching opportunity at one of the small circle of institutions considered national powers in football, the defensive-oriented coach didn't have to think too long about who he wanted to structure his offense.

"It wasn't instant," Stoops recalled about how long it took him to decide on Kentucky assistant Mike Leach as his offensive coordinator, "but it didn't take too long. In my time at Florida, I knew the kind of talent we had and I knew the kind of talent [Kentucky] had, and I was just awfully impressed by what they were able to accomplish.

"Hal Mumme wasn't going anywhere," Stoops said of Kentucky's head coach, "so I decided to get his offensive coordinator."

The combination of a versatile defense and the high-octane offense Leach brought with him—a bizarre concoction that was part run-and-shoot, part BYU boilerplate, and part spread, which they called the air raid offense—brought a championship to Oklahoma in Stoops's second season at Norman. By then Leach had been hired away to run the program at Texas Tech, but his offense remained.

At first sight, Stoops was knocked out by the Mumme-Leach offense.

In 1996, Stoops's first year at Florida, the easiest game by far on the schedule—which included victories over Louisiana-Lafayette (55–21) and Georgia Southern (62–14)—was an SEC game at home against Kentucky, a 65–0 victory. It was Florida's only shutout of the season and the most points it scored in a single game.

The next year—the first season for Mumme and Leach at Kentucky—the Gators recorded a 55–28 victory, and they prevailed again the next year, 51–35. The first time around,

Mumme's offense scored more points against Florida than anyone other than Georgia and Florida State. The second year, nobody scored as much as Kentucky in games against Florida.

Stoops knew what Kentucky had before Mumme got there and after he got there. That's what made him want to hire Mike Leach. "We just had a heck of a time figuring them out," Stoops said. "I remember thinking what kind of trouble they could cause if they had an equal level of talent. I wanted that kind of offense on my side."

The combustible stew of aggressive emotion that Erickson wanted to see in his players' eyes had its consequences. He was told after the 1989 championship that, though the team's public comportment had improved, it needed to get better, and he said he would endeavor to do just that. He wanted to know more about his players and their backgrounds, so he found his way to some of the clubs and nightspots Hurricanes were known to visit.

Erickson met and became friends with Luther Campbell, the manager and eventual lead singer of the hip-hop group 2 Live Crew, whose most popular album, *As Nasty as They Wanna Be*, included sexually explicit lyrics that prompted a lawsuit to get it removed from the airwaves. Campbell and his group were just like the Miami football team in the sense that their musical expression upset those who would set themselves up as moral guardians for youth in the same way the 'Canes antics sent college football rules committees into executive session. "Luther was a good guy," Erickson said. "He was in that cultural mix with our players and after I got to know him and realized what he was about, I didn't have a problem with him like some people did."

That in itself was an affront to some. They wanted Erickson to ban players from associating with Campbell, from being in those clubs and associating themselves with hip-hop culture. To Erickson, it was no different than a coach back home telling him to stay of the neighborhoods where the Swedes hung out—they were trouble. Those were his people, just as Campbell and company were just another form of expression in a free society. Players appreciated Erickson's interest and judgment, but it didn't help his image or that of the football program.

Far worse were the federal crimes taking place within the university's financial aid department. Tony Russell, an academic adviser hired in 1989, eventually pleaded guilty in 1994 to assisting more than eighty scholarship athletes—including fifty-seven football players—in falsifying Pell Grant applications in exchange for kickbacks from the players. Federal officials referred to it as "perhaps the largest centralized fraud . . . ever committed in the history of the Pell Grant program."

None of it had anything to do with Erickson, who didn't know Russell—the office was located in a different building on campus—and had nothing to do with his hiring, but along with a handful of other incidents, it was another big smudge on the image. Before he left Miami for Seattle to coach the NFL's Seahawks in 1995, Erickson was also accused in the media of looking the other way when it came to drug-testing football players.

"Of all the stuff that people said about us, that was the one that still amazes me," Erickson said of the drug-testing rumors.

In the first place, the University of Miami didn't have a drug-testing policy at the time, and while we did test some players, we were the only ones there who were testing.

You didn't know what policies were from day to day because of the revolving door in administration. Sam hired me, then he left the second year [in December 1990] and Dave Maggard came in [1991–93], and then he left and Paul [Dee] took over when Maggard left; each time there were new rules, different ways of doing things, and the messages through the chain of command were never clear because the chain of command seemed to be in constant turnover.

But I know one thing, we were the only ones drug testing at a time when they were accusing us of going against university drug-testing policies that didn't exist.

If I wouldn't have been there and experienced it myself, I wouldn't have believed that you could get accused of not drug testing your players when you were actually the only one in the athletic department who *was* testing players.

It was almost enough to take the fun out of winning, so after six record-setting seasons, two national championships, and numerous national awards won by his players, Erickson accepted an offer to go back home and coach the Seahawks. He lasted through four of the most turbulent years that any franchise experienced in the decade of the 1990s. Owner Ken Behring had purchased the team from the Nordstrom family, who brought pro football to Seattle in 1976. A Northern California real estate developer, Behring had previously named former agent Mike Blatt as interim general manager, a short stint that ended when Blatt was tried on a murder-for-hire charge.

Red flags? Oh, there were several, but it was home, paid more money, and they had talked about doing things right with the Seahawks, so Erickson decided to see what it was like being an NFL coach, figuring he'd been sufficiently prepared by the constant administrative changes and communication breakdowns that existed at Miami.

Turned out he was wrong about that.

After Erickson came in, Behring began lobbying for a new stadium, alleging the Kingdome was inadequate and unsafe. At one point Behring threatened to move the team to Los Angeles and had equipment physically moved to Southern California in the off-season before the league stepped in. After stripping the team of personnel by slashing costs, Behring sold the Seahawks to Microsoft cofounder Paul Allen, who then installed Bob Whitsitt as general manager.

Erickson and Whitsitt shared a Seattle background, but Whitsitt knew nothing about football, having made his mark in sports as a pro basketball general manager, first in Seattle with the Sonics, then later in Portland with the Allen-owned Trail Blazers. "From the first day we met, Bob gave me the feeling he wanted me out," Erickson said. "He seemed like a decent-enough guy, I just think when Paul got in there, he wanted to make some changes, clean things up and get going again, but they just didn't know what they really wanted to do for a while. I probably represented bad things from the past, I guess."

There was plenty of bad stuff to dwell on. Erickson inherited a team that had been 14-34 the previous three seasons, with a series of bungled draft choices. His quarterback was Rick Mirer, a first-round draft choice the year before who wound up as a career-long backup in the NFL. Erickson found quarterbacks wherever he could; he invited Jon Kitna to camp after attending an NAIA playoff game to watch his sister's son play running back for Central Washington University, where Kitna was the quarterback.

Kitna played for Seattle, as did John Friesz, a former Idaho quarterback Erickson knew, and he closed out with aging Warren Moon in his spread offense. There were some high points, like the time Friesz replaced Mirer in the second half and led Seattle from a twenty-point deficit to a win in Denver against the Broncos and John Elway, and there were low points, like the time the Seahawks lost on the road to the New York Jets, 32–31.

That game, decided in the final seconds on a dive toward the goal line by quarterback Vinny Testaverde, cost the Seahawks a likely playoff berth and also prompted a rules change. Testaverde came up clearly short of the goal line, but instant replay was not used to correct the call in 1998 and the play was allowed to stand. By the time the football season started in 1999, instant replay was a part of the game and Erickson was back in college football.

The spread was infiltrating college football with alarming momentum by the time Erickson left Miami in 1995. He had done something no Miami coach before or since has been able to match — two championships in the first three seasons, four championships played for in six years with a 63-9 record. Never mind that the social drama stirred up around the Miami players stole most of the headlines; what Erickson's teams did on the field hasn't since been matched by anyone, and to not recognize the full blossom of the spread offense as a major contributor would be to not see the forest for the trees in terms of the revolution that was taking place in offensive strategy.

Mike Price, Erickson's former high school teammate, was coaching Ryan Leaf into a Rose Bowl quarterback at Washington State, and Joe Tiller, the old Washington State coaching friend of Jack Elway and Erickson, took the spread offense to Purdue and the Big 10 in 1997, the same year Mumme went to Kentucky. Tiller promised to turn the Big 10 into a spread offense conference and did exactly that at a time when the tradition-rich SEC was being convulsed by Mumme's approach at Kentucky.

"He was the guy who really started that whole trend in the Big 10," said former Notre Dame coach Bob Davie. "I know, because we played them every year. They were no huddle, they would spread you out all over the field, and everyone was skeptical about it when he got there. They talked about the cold weather in November, the tradition in the conference of running the ball, the toughness, all the things they said wouldn't allow that offense to be successful.

"Well, they were all wrong. Everybody in the Big 10 eventually ran the spread, or at least had it available for certain situations."

Around that time, a couple of young coaches with big ideas were brainstorming the wave of the future at Notre Dame.

While working as defensive coordinator for coach Lou Holtz, Davie got to know Urban Meyer, hired from Colorado State by Holtz to coach running backs. After Holtz left, Davie was named head coach in '97 and he hired Kevin Rogers from Syracuse in 1999 as offensive coordinator, impressed with the work Rogers had done in the Orange offense using the running and passing talents of quarterback Donovan McNabb. Rogers brought Dan Mullen with him from Syracuse as a graduate assistant.

Mullen and Meyer hit it off right away. "We kicked around ideas, no question," Mullen said. "You have a couple of guys wanting to try different things, just brainstorming basically, but we got along, I guess that's the main thing—we put up with each other."

Davie, through Meyer and Mullen, was exploring different ways to use the quarterback at Notre Dame with Jarious Jackson, a good runner who broke several single-season passing marks for the Irish, and Carlyle Holiday, a highly recruited running quarterback from Texas.

They borrowed some of the Syracuse playbook for McNabb, played with some new ideas of their own, and earned a Bowl

Championship Series bowl bid in 2000 with a 9-3 team that went to the Fiesta Bowl and took a hellacious thumping from Oregon State, coached then by Erickson. Notre Dame's success in 2000 came on the heels of a 5-7 record the previous year, and despite the crushing end, it attracted enough attention that Meyer was hired to coach at Bowling Green. He took Mullen with him as his offensive coordinator.

It was a good time to be at the Ohio school and not at Notre Dame. The Irish slumped back to 5-6 and Davie was fired, while Meyer and Mullen caught fire with the Falcons, turning a team that was 2-9 the previous season into an 8-3 team, the biggest turnaround of the year among bowl-division schools.

The Meyer-Mullen spread offense took flight again in 2002 with a 9-3 record that included wins of 51–28 over Missouri and 39–16 over Kansas and scoreboard busters like the 72–21 rout of Ohio and the 63–21 trampling of Eastern Michigan. Everybody was noticing Bowling Green, and how often have you been able to say that in the past fifty years?

Utah did something about it, hiring the Meyer-Mullen coaching team in 2003 to resuscitate a program that had fallen to 5-6 in Coach Ron McBride's thirteenth year. They inherited quarterback Alex Smith and transformed the Utes into one of the national college football talking points for the 2003 and 2004 seasons, using an exotic blend of formations, motion, and subterfuge to confuse defenses—and reminding coaches everywhere about the possibilities of the spread offense. Utah was 10-2 the first year and 12-0 the second, which was enough for Florida to hire Meyer.

At that point, the spread offense, popping up in personnel groupings here and there, was about to make its official, no-holds-barred debut with a winning program in the SEC. That could have happened a year earlier. Alabama athletic director Mal Moore—the old Montana State assistant, thanks to Jim Sweeney's friendship with Bear Bryant—hired Washington State's Mike Price to coach the Crimson Tide in late 2002. A night in a topless bar during a trip to Pensacola, Florida, that following spring, with extravagant charges tacked on to Price's room later that night, got him fired before he ever coached a game. So the spread offense that derailed an Alabama championship after the '89 season almost, but not quite, became the new Alabama offense.

The first time Meyer and Mullen glimpsed the spread was in 1999, when they visited the University of Louisville for a day to talk with offensive coordinator Scott Linehan, who they heard was doing some creative things offensively. "I think we stayed for about a week," Meyer said in a 2008 interview. "That got us talking and we also liked a lot of what [quarterback] Michael Bishop was doing for [Coach] Bill Snyder at Kansas State. We didn't have a playbook or anything, but we had a lot of ideas."

Meyer said he first remembered seeing the spread when he was an assistant at Colorado State and watched Michael Bishop at quarterback for Kansas State, but his memory was playing tricks on him. Bishop started for Coach Bill Snyder in 1997, two years after Meyer left Colorado State, although it's true that Snyder was experimenting with running the quarterback out of a spread concept almost a decade before it caught on in the NCAA.

Experimenting with the read option as a part of the quarterback's routine came to Snyder out of necessity. That happened to a lot of coaches at Kansas State over the years, but the rest of them weren't Bill Snyder. Thanks to a swarming defense he developed at Kansas State with a couple of skilled defensive coaches named Bob Stoops and Jim Leavitt, who shared the coordinator's role, the Wildcats were stopping the run throughout the Big 12 Conference, which was good, but they were having trouble running their own offense in practice against their defense. Stoops had been the linebackers coach for Snyder in his remarkable makeover that reconstructed a canvas-backed program that ranked among the nation's worst into one that challenged the best in the conference.

Under Snyder, Kansas State football was turned into a beast because of that suffocating defense, which stuffed the line of scrimmage and dared teams to pass into a single-safety secondary. That defense made everything happen at Kansas State. It enabled the Wildcats to stand up and be counted. Then the offense kicked in with a series of versatile quarterbacks like Matt Miller, Michael Bishop, Jonathon Beasley, and Ell Roberson.

"Our defense created uneven matchups for others and for us," Snyder said. "We realized the only way we could get to even or create an uneven matchup for the offense was to utilize the quarterback in the running game. That's where it all came from."

Just as Jack Neumeier's frustration against quicker, more athletic teams prompted his interest in spreading defenses, Snyder's realization opened up his offense. "It really became a doorway for us," Snyder said of the spread offense. "It gives you a great amount of versatility and a variety of ways to go in recruiting. You can take many different skill sets and find ways to use them effectively within the framework of these concepts."

Bishop could run and throw, and at the end of the 1997 season he won a battle with Syracuse and McNabb in the Fiesta Bowl. Bishop completed fourteen of twenty-three passes for 317 yards and four touchdowns and he ran fifteen times for 73 yards and another TD in a 35–18 win over the Orange.

When Meyer and Mullen visited Linehan at Louisville, they didn't realize they were talking offensive concepts with one of the first quarterbacks who played in a true spread offense in college football. What they knew was that the schemes, the structures they saw for the spread, were expanding their football consciousness in an exponential fashion.

"We couldn't stop talking about it and thinking about it," said Mullen in a 2009 interview. "It wasn't something we were going to bring to Notre Dame, but we would throw some ideas [at Davie] from time to time just to rattle his cage a little."

"It wasn't a distraction," Davie said of the Myer-Mullen suggestions. "I was with them on a lot of the stuff they were talking about but we were invested in what we were doing. Those guys were stereotypes, two young assistants full of ideas, that's what you want on your staff."

Meyer was a full generation behind the birth of the spread when he met Linehan, who quarterbacked the offense for Erickson at Idaho in 1984, seventeen years before Meyer became a head coach, but he immediately discerned the potential of the design because he grasped the challenge it brought to defenses.

"When you talk about basketball on grass, you're talking about one-on-one tackling all over the field," Davie said. "The spread has virtually eliminated gang tackling for the simple reason that your defense is literally spread out—it's too far between you and the rest of your guys out there, you're on your own, so you better make that one-on-one tackle."

Bo Schembechler might be turning over in his grave. It was a good thing that he wasn't around to see the spread offense—run by Appalachian State, no less—that he once derided as a gimmick defeat his Michigan Wolverines. It might have been too much to bear had he been around when the school hired Rich Rodriguez to bring the spread to Ann Arbor.

Defenses prepare for the spread offense with multiple personnel packages that complicate the preparation of coordinators who really have no other alternative. Finally, almost thirty years after Jack Elway and Dennis Erickson brought the spread offense to major college football, defenses have caught up.

Almost.

14

Spirit of a New Millennium (2000s)

In the second half of the twentieth century, no two major college football programs were perceived as more unlikely places to win than Kansas State and Oregon State. Bill Snyder largely turned around Kansas State by the 1990s, and in 2000 football got up and made noise like never before in Corvallis, Oregon.

For longtime Oregon State fans, having a winning season was a little like waking up in a dream. The last time a team in that idyllic, misty-evergreen-mornings town had consecutive winning seasons was during the Nixon administration, 1969 and 1970. That's when Dee Andros was head coach and Oregon State was a no-nonsense team that gave every opponent sleepless nights while preparing to meet the physically overpowering and defensively ruthless Beavers. The defense posed such a challenge it gained the nickname the Black Bandits of Benton County and earned a reputation as the nastiest crew on the West Coast.

Andros was a true American hero, a Marine who fought for a month on Iwo Jima and personally witnessed the triumphant flag-raising there before returning to play football for Bud Wilkinson at Oklahoma and then going into coaching at Idaho and Oregon State. Though he knew only one way to coach, Andros was no relic of the past. When he saw

Erickson's spread offense take apart his Beavers and Coach Joe Avezzano, Andros believed it was the future of offensive football and tried, unsuccessfully, to hire Erickson after the firing of Avezzano in 1984. Andros saw the game change beginning in 1971, when Oregon State football began careening down the side of a seemingly endless hill of despair that would last for twenty-eight consecutive losing seasons.

The way out at Corvallis, just as it had been at Kansas State, the nation's other most hapless major college football program, was provided by the spread offense. The transformation at Oregon State came not from an exploratory spread that exploited a tough quarterback's running ability but from the original spread design based on Erickson's twenty-year history in the offense. It began when Erickson picked up the phone one day in Seattle and called Director of Athletics Mitch Barnhart, inquiring about the Beavers' coaching vacancy.

The Seahawks had just fired Erickson after four years when his record was two wins under .500. Not a great shock that a so-so record like that would get an NFL coach fired, but in Erickson's case, had the ownership situation been known ahead of time, nobody would have predicted the team would be on the verge of playoffs in his fourth year.

Oregon State had just lost Mike Riley to the San Diego Chargers after Riley had some progress. His 1997 team was 3-8, but they improved to 5-6 in '98, winning four of their last five games. It had been twenty-seven years since any Oregon State team had won five games.

Erickson called Barnhart about the opening and two days later he was a Pac-10 head coach once again. His quarterback was a five-foot-ten headstrong kid named Jonathan Smith and his running back was Ken Simonton, all of five-eight, but Riley had recruited some talent on defense as well as a talented receiver, T. J. Houshmandzadeh.

In Erickson's first year Oregon State went 7-5, a watershed event for the university after decades of failure. The anticipation for back-to-back winning seasons in 2000 was like a joyous virus that swept through the Willamette Valley.

That summer before his second season, Erickson had dispatched assistant coach Eric Yarber to look for talent in the Los Angeles area and Yarber found someone special. Chad Johnson had attended Erickson's football camps in Miami years earlier, then bounced around at a couple of different colleges, his classroom dedication no match for his football desires. He was in Southern California with one remaining year of college eligibility when a scout friend of Erickson's alerted Yarber.

Johnson had everything coaches look for in a receiver, from height (six-one), to weight (195), to speed (sub-4.5 40 speed), but his hands were well beyond what coaches usually find in college. "I was watching him catching passes one day and he was running a slant when the ball was thrown behind him," Yarber said. "Without breaking stride, he stuck out that backside arm, caught it in his hand like Spider-Man, and pulled it in. I called Dennis as soon as I could and said, 'We have to find a way to get this guy into school.'"

Johnson had to take classes all summer to gain eligibility. Yarber walked across campus five days a week to get updates from staff members in touch with Johnson's instructors in Southern California and from admission department personnel who were trying to untangle a knot of credits from other schools. Johnson became eligible, got to campus, and immediately struggled with hanging on to the ball.

In the third game of the season, at home against San Diego State, Smith lobbed a pass to Johnson in the end zone that he caught for a touchdown. He came running to the sidelines with the ball in his hands, held tightly. "He had a huge smile and tears were running down his cheeks like the dam just broke," said Yarber. "Everything opened up after that."

Johnson and Houshmandzadeh stretched defenses apart, Simonton was a devastating, shifty inside runner, and the Oregon State defense played with the kind of snarl Erickson hadn't seen since Miami. "I wanted to see the (Miami) kind of effort and intensity they put into every practice, because they played like that every day, so I knew it was possible, and from then on, I knew you could coach that into players; that's the approach we took in Corvallis," he said.

At Miami, it was always interpreted as arrogance; at Oregon State the same approach came across in media reports as evidence of an undisciplined team. Miami showed Erickson that football is best played right at the edge of emotional intensity, to the point that some opponents won't be prepared or willing to match that edge and will back off. The downside of this approach is that it results in more penalties than you would get with teams that don't rise to that emotional level, but Erickson's approach was to take it to the edge and coach smart play that avoids penalties rather than to hold back emotion in hopes it will come out when needed.

Smith said Erickson had that team in the palm of his hand. "We all liked Riley, really liked him," Smith said, "but it was different with Erickson. Riley was one of the guys, and when he would come in the locker room to talk to us, we'd know he was there, but guys would be yakking and laughing and he'd have to tell us to be quiet.

"When Erickson walked in the room, he had that kind of swagger about him and it would fall silent, immediately," Smith said. "We all knew what he had done at Miami and we all heard him the first day he was hired when he said his goal was to win at least ten games and go to the BCS. We believed every word he said."

In 2000 it all happened with the spread offense and a nasty defense. Oregon State went 11-1, losing only at Washington, by three points when a late field goal drifted wide of the goalpost. When the Beavers beat Oregon, 23–13, in the final regular-season game to win ten games for the first time in school history, the stands emptied onto the field and fans stomped away generations of football misery.

After the 2000 regular season, the Fiesta Bowl committee had its choice of opponents due to a complicated system of awarding matchups that involved the new Bowl Championship Series. Virginia Tech, with the spectacularly gifted Michael Vick at quarterback, was rated fifth in the BCS selection process. Oregon State, cochampions of the Pacific-10 Conference—their first such accomplishment since the 1964 season, when Erickson was a junior in high school—was rated sixth. Notre Dame, which started 2-2 but rallied to finish the regular season 9-2, was ranked eleventh. There had been speculation that the Fiesta Bowl might bypass Oregon State, as Pac-10 rival Washington had been granted a berth in the Rose Bowl, another BCS bowl—the five BCS bowls were averaging payout of $12 million per team that year—but Pac-10 commissioner Tom Hanson threatened to pull the conference out of the BCS entirely if Oregon State was denied a Fiesta Bowl opportunity.

Officially pressured or not, the Fiesta Bowl invited Oregon State, then surprised Virginia Tech by selecting Notre Dame as its opponent. The rising phenomenon Michael Vick couldn't match the television ratings promise that Notre Dame would deliver, regardless of the opponent. All week long leading up to the game, Oregon State felt like uninvited guests at someone else's party.

Erickson sensed something was about to break because he'd been through this before. In his second year at Miami the Hurricanes had lost just once—to Notre Dame—and didn't get an invitation to play for a national title. School president Tad Foote was also scolding them for what he perceived to be unseemly behavior. Then, when they arrived in the Cotton Bowl to play Texas, Miami players felt that they were treated like second-class citizens, just as they had a few years earlier in Arizona for the national championship game against Penn State.

A similar set of circumstances unfolded in Arizona for the Fiesta Bowl when Oregon State players and fans were made to feel as though they should be happy to have second billing to Notre Dame. At dinners, press gatherings, and other mandatory Fiesta Bowl functions, Notre Dame always seemed to be pirouetting in the middle of the dance floor while the traveling party from the Willamette Valley was encouraged to enjoy themselves off to the side, out of the way.

As Miami had done earlier in the Cotton Bowl, Oregon State played an explosive game against the Irish, complete with penalty flags. Quarterback Jonathan Smith threw for 305 yards and three touchdowns and led Oregon State to a 41–9 rout in a game in which Chad Johnson had two touchdown receptions and future Cincinnati teammate T. J. Houshmandzadeh caught the other scoring pass.

"Probably coaches say this a lot," Erickson observed, "but at the end of the season, I doubt any team in the country was playing any better. You wouldn't have wanted to draw Oregon State in a playoff, if they had one back then."

Oregon State's aggressive defense began attracting penalties. Assistant coach Dan Cozzetto recalled hearing Erickson's dry wit come through the headsets when an unnecessary penalty was called. "They were going wild throwing flags. At one point, Dennis walked out about 10 yards on the field, gets the attention of the guy who made the call, and says, 'If you guys don't stop blowing so many whistles, I'm going to turn these players loose.'

"Classic Erickson," Cozzetto said. "Yeah, there were a lot of penalties, and some bad ones, in the first half, but it wasn't like that in the second half; didn't matter, they kept throwing flags."

The 2000 season and that game against Notre Dame changed the perception of Oregon State football. In four years, Oregon State went 31-17 under Erickson. Before he passed away in 2003, Andros finally got to see Erickson bring the spread to Corvallis for the school's most successful season. A sideline legend in Corvallis, Andros had the nickname "The Great Pumpkin" bestowed on him by Spokane newspaper columnist Harry Missildine because of his large midsection and the appearance he took on in that orange Beavers windbreaker. The ex-Marine lived long enough to observe the full transformation of the football program.

Andros said in an interview in 1999 that, while watching Erickson's Vandals turn away Oregon State in 1984, he noticed how Erickson would call plays and know what was going to happen. Often, as soon as the ball was snapped and Erickson got a glimpse at the defense, he would turn his back on the game and consult his play chart for the next call as quarterback Scott Linehan would throw another completion into the confused Oregon State defense.

"He was in complete control of that football team," Andros said. "As a former coach, that's what impressed me so much. He knew what was going to happen out there and that team responded to him, they gang-tackled, they swarmed the football on defense, and they spread us out and picked us apart on offense with personnel that wasn't as good as ours.

"I wanted to see him on our sidelines, coaching the Oregon State football team," Andros said. "It took a while, but it finally happened."

A year after Idaho beat the Beavers, Andros lobbied for Erickson but he was outvoted and the OSU board hired Dave Kragthorpe, a BYU coaching disciple of LaVell Edwards who went 17-49-8 in six years before he was fired. Who knows how different college football might have been had Oregon State hired Erickson in 1985.

In May 2009 ESPN football analyst Bob Davie was describing film of Florida's offense from the 2008 season and the direction that the hybrid no-huddle, spread offenses had taken the game of football. "I'll tell you what, you better start breaking this down over the summer if you're going to play Florida," Davie said of the complexity of offensive packages that had been installed by Gators coach Urban Meyer. "What [Meyer] does, the packages he puts together, are so unorthodox, it just really looks very, very different and it takes time—a lot of time—to try to figure out what he's doing.

"We used to have to do that in the summer to sort out what triple-option teams were doing," Davie said. "Now Urban is doing that with his spread. Because he has all these hybrid players—players who line up at one position but really play like another position—you can't just say, 'When they're in four wides, we'll do this,' because one of those four might really be a running back and another might be a tight end, so you might send out a personnel group to play against four wides that, in actuality, is only two wides; you might not have the right personnel out there."

That's what Meyer means when he talks about how it all comes down to personnel. The spread is, as it always was from the time Jack Neumeier first considered it watching a high school basketball game, about a *concept*, not about plays. The plays can be passed around from offense to offense and be meaningless based on the players running those plays.

Your team's personnel tells you which small handful of running and passing plays you need in your offense. The rest of it is a matter of confusing the defense with an array of personnel packages and formations that confounds preparation.

Prior to his team's 2012 season opener against Boise State, Michigan State coach Mark Dantonio said that in preparation for the game his defensive staff had identified 178 different formations used by the Broncos. Not like it was when Bob Davie ran the same twenty-nine defenses against an opponent. Now the best a defense can do is come up with many different looks to confuse the quarterback when he tries to get an idea whether he'll be blitzed on the play.

It doesn't seem to happen as much as it did in the past, but it is still possible to have a strong defense and a wide-open spread offense at the same time. You just can't use the same yardstick as in the past. You will be repeatedly disappointed if you're looking for a shutout.

Kansas State became an example of the spread offense combining with a muscular and agile defense to make history when the Wildcats began terrorizing the Big 12 Conference with Michael Bishop as their running and passing quarterback. The Wildcats were a perennial college football loser that was given new life, but they aren't the only example. Other schools switched from a traditional power game to a spread-based attack, some with more efficiency than others, but there was no longer any question that the spread offense had changed the way college football was being played. The accent was on speed, one-on-one match-ups all over the field, and making the defense position itself where the offense dictated. The game had been turned inside out.

For all its tactical appeal to coaches, for the seductive big-play opportunities it offers to athletes, and for all the on-field success teams have had with the spread offense, let's not fool ourselves, it's not going to inoculate them from failure. It is, at one level in the big picture of Thinking Man's Football, just another way to get the job done. Teams are still running the single wing and the Delaware wing-T and winning with it at the high school and college levels. The wishbone has had some resurgence with a few updates at Georgia Tech, Army, and other schools.

The spread is not a panacea for failure, it is only another design, but that observable fact says a lot about the ground it has covered in the forty years since it was first used at a suburban Los Angeles high school. At the time it was considered a gimmick, a short-lived nuisance offense that would come and go before anyone had to deal with it in a serious way.

Clearly that initial reaction by a broad range of coaches and media skeptics missed its mark, wildly. The thing Jack Neumeier and Jack Elway thought about the spread—that it wasn't just a series of plays but a completely different strategic context in which to play the game—has proven to be the most progressive and utilitarian vision for football since the 1960s. Moreover, most coaches today agree that the popularity of the spread, which has swamped the wishbone, the veer, and derivatives of those two option-based attacks in terms of its immersion throughout the game, from pros to peewees, won't diminish anytime soon.

It has become a natural fit culturally because of its appeal to athletes who might otherwise have played basketball or baseball. The spread saturated the game because it had the effect, singular to the other major sports, of being attractive to play on a year-round basis. Taller, more agile kids who might have played basketball have instead gravitated to the spread, as have baseball players and track athletes. More than with the power or the option-based offenses, players can envision themselves in the spread from the first moment they see it on a football field.

The spread offense was an enticing recruiting tool from its very inception, the statistical production often breaking charts and rewriting passing records wherever it was used. But it still can get you fired. People who were once seen at the vanguard of the offense in some regions as it entered football's bloodstream in the 1980s and '90s have tumbled and fallen at times. Some get up, others struggle, but try to find one of the true believers from the '80s or '90s who gave it up and went to another system. You might look a long time before you find your guy.

Along the way, schools like Florida, Oklahoma, Texas, West Virginia, Purdue, Texas Tech, Auburn, Oregon, and others that used the offense to win big have been held up as notable practitioners. Others, like Kansas State, that experienced early and serious curiosity with the various permutations of the offense, have been less recognized.

To some coaches, invested with decades of teaching a certain way of playing football, change feels like a threat to their future. It's one thing to change when you're UTEP or Northwestern or any number of schools that don't have a long history of success; it's another animal altogether when you represent the antithesis of everything that a place like Auburn has projected to the college football world. Auburn is perhaps the best example of the turmoil and angst that can be generated when the spread is considered by a program with a traditional approach and a fan base—and coaching staff—that wants to remain faithful to symbols of past glory.

Pat Dye had led Auburn to ninety-nine wins in twelve seasons, encouraging the fan base with great running backs, none more storied than Heisman Trophy–winner Bo Jackson. Dye's run came to an end when he was connected to NCAA rules violations. He was followed by Terry Bowden, son of Florida State legend Bobby Bowden. The young coach inherited a program on probation and, while ineligible for the SEC title because of the sanctions, he coached Auburn to an 11-0 record in his first season. He was 20-1-1 after two years and then came a gradual slide in recruiting. Off-field issues led him to resign after a 1-5 start in 1998.

Tommy Tuberville, the linebackers coach Erickson kept on when he took over at Miami, jumped from his job at Mississippi to become the replacement for Terry Bowden. He was just 5-6 in his first season, then went to the SEC championship game in 2000 after beating Alabama in Tuscaloosa. Tuberville kept them going strong, fashioning a flawless 13-0 record in 2004 that wasn't good enough to win the votes that would have given them a share of the national championship, but by 2007 the fan base was restless.

In came Tony Franklin, an instrumental figure in the escalation of the spread offense throughout the Southeast. By the time he was hired by Auburn, Franklin had helped install Mumme's offense at Kentucky and was orchestrating ways for Troy to score points in bunches when Tuberville brought him in.

Tuberville was and remains—at Cincinnati these days—a defensive coach. He wants to run the ball and he wants to stop your team from doing the same. But at tradition-rich Auburn, a school drenched in running-football lore with the likes of former backs Bo Jackson, Stephen Davis, James Brooks, Joe Cribbs, and others, the offense had become stagnant by 2007.

From his time as a young coach on Erickson's staff at Miami, dating back to 1989, Tuberville knew the inherent potency of a spread offense run properly. He knew it could be productive on the ground and through the air and he felt he needed an upgrade after the regular season ended with an 8-4 record, including 5-3 in the conference and the sixth consecutive victory over rival Alabama, leaving the Tigers short of where much of the fan base thought they should be.

After the Iron Bowl Tuberville fired offensive coordinator Al Borges and brought in Franklin to introduce the spread, just eight days before a 2007 bowl game in the Georgia Dome against Clemson. At the time, Clemson was ranked ninth nationally in NCAA defensive statistics and Franklin's late inclusion left the unmistakable impression that Auburn's offensive approach was in turmoil.

Not much was expected leading up to the game. Tuberville undersold the effect of the new addition to his offensive staff because of the lack of preparation time he had with his new hire, but the bowl game results were as surprising as they were impressive. Auburn topped its season's best in all offensive categories with 423 yards (including 190 rushing) and ran an eleven-year-high ninety offensive plays in a 23–20 overtime victory. For tradition's sake, that game marked a detour for Auburn, which had built a modern framework around the belief in, and effective use of, a no-nonsense running game.

Hiring Franklin sent shock waves through the fan base and, more importantly, through the staff of Tuberville's assistants. The presumption was that the proud running tradition of Auburn football was about to undergo a drastic makeover.

"I would love to say Auburn is still a power running team," Pat Dye told the Associated Press in the off-season following the bowl victory over Clemson, "but the fact of life today is that, unless you can be guaranteed all the best players—better than anyone else in the SEC—on a yearly basis so that you can dictate to everyone else how the game will be played based on talent, the best thing you can do is play the spread.

"There isn't anybody in this day and age who's going to get all the best players," Dye said. "That's just a fact of life, so you better be playing the spread."

Dye's concept of the spread as some magic eraser of offensive ills was misguided and uninformed. The spread cannot disguise a lack of talent, but it can help equalize a talent disparity when a coaching staff is committed to the offense.

For instance, a college team with capable, if not exceptional, offensive talent can commit to a no-huddle spread offense, signal plays in from the bench, and run plays fifteen seconds after the ball is spotted from the previous play. It might be up against a bigger, stronger, and faster defense, but without the ability to make personnel-package substitutions, that defense is going to get winded.

Utah recorded a 12-0 season in 2008 after it defeated Alabama, 31–17, in the Sugar Bowl behind a spread offense led by quarterback Brian Johnson. The offense was essentially the same used by Coach Urban Meyer a few years earlier and it was impossible, watching the game, not to notice how quickly the Utes were running plays in roaring off to a 21–0 lead.

This was no fluke victory. It was a win over a team that had gone 12-0 in the Southeastern Conference before losing the conference championship game to Florida. Alabama had better players but it was caught flat-footed at times, trying to make personnel changes on defense when the ball was snapped. By the fourth quarter Alabama was still in the game, it still had a chance to win, but the Crimson Tide was fatigued from the pace of the game.

Utah was able to do that because it had a coaching staff and a roster full of players that had been invested in the spread offense for years. The seniors on the Utes had played in no other style of offense throughout their collegiate careers and the coaching staff had been at it long enough to fully grasp the spread's various advantages.

Tony Franklin's experience at Auburn rings like a cautionary tale from most any form of structured endeavor. Like following a legend, it's usually preferable to be the second innovator in a time of change if everyone isn't on the bandwagon.

They weren't on the bandwagon at Auburn. There was only so much Franklin could do in the limited time available to him before the bowl game, but on the coaching staff there was a generalized fear of Franklin possibly being successful and what it might mean for everyone else.

In retrospect, Franklin felt he was perceived as an unwanted outsider even before the Clemson game. "Everybody was nice to me when I got there," Franklin said,

> but away from the fans and the media I was hearing things early on. When we got on the bus to ride over to the [Clemson] game, I started walking down the aisle—I've always sat in among the players on the bus—but the coaches said, "No, no, that's your seat over there."
>
> They were pointing to an aisle seat up front and I thought it was kind of weird that they would have certain seats all picked out, but no big deal, I sat there. I heard some kind of giggling and I thought I heard something about "dead man's seat," but I wasn't sure where it came from.

Auburn had a succession of offensive coaches in the Tuberville era. He brought Noel Mazzone with him from his previous job at Mississippi, but after two seasons, Tuberville moved Mazzone out in favor of Bobby Petrino, who lasted just one year before he took a head-coaching job at Louisville. Petrino was replaced by Hugh Nall, then when his work wasn't what Tuberville wanted, Nall was moved to the offensive line and Al Borges was hired to be the new offensive coordinator. Borges was run off for Franklin, then halfway through the 2008 season, with the spread offense little more than an unused concept, Franklin was fired. Borges, Nall, Petrino, and Mazzone all had sat where they directed Franklin, in the dead man's seat.

"I really didn't think about it much after we won that Clemson game," Franklin said, "but I could tell in spring ball we didn't have everybody on board. Later, I heard that dead man's seat comment again. I would hear things from the other coaches that they had to know I was hearing that let me know what was going on.

"I would hear, 'Better to sacrifice one than to lose the whole staff,' those kinds of things," he said. "It was a matter of them not believing in it, not wanting to give it an honest shot. We never ran the spread at Auburn, it never had a chance."

Exactly what happened to Tony Franklin in granular detail at Auburn is beside the point, except to say it seemed as though he was brought into a somewhat hostile environment created by the rest of the staff. Franklin was the only one on the staff invested in his offensive system and because he was separate from the others, he needed time to coach the rest of the coaches, to build a level of familiarity with them, but that never happened. A case could be made that Tuberville lost control of his staff or that he had decided to step down at the end of the season and allowed Franklin to be run into the ditch. How much of Franklin's problems of assimilation on the staff started with his own personality and to what extent Tuberville's lack of leadership in terms of making it clear that Franklin's system needed to be supported will never be completely understood.

But it is clear that the spread arrived at the Auburn University football program as a threat to Auburn tradition and

Auburn tradition won the battle, if not the war. The over-arching irony is that three years later, with Tuberville and the previous staff gone, Auburn recorded a perfect season, beat Alabama again the year after the Tide had won a national championship, quarterback Cam Newton won the Heisman Trophy, and all of it came out of an up-tempo, no-huddle spread offense.

"It was a bad situation, the coaching staff wasn't behind the concepts I was bringing in," Franklin said of his brief time at Auburn. "I thought I had Tuberville's support, I mean, he hired me, but I never had a relationship with him. We didn't have, really, any meaningful conversations. In all the time I was there, I talked to Tommy maybe an hour and a half, total."

On October 8, 2008, Tuberville fired Franklin with the Auburn offense ranked 104th nationally. Tuberville told the Associated Press that Franklin's dismissal was "not going to change our philosophy. This is a good offense. Our guys like it. They understand it. They're getting better at it."

Upon reflection, it was a remarkable statement. A school with a long-standing tradition of running the ball brings in an offensive coordinator—its fifth in ten years—invested in a system with a different look and feel, yet that system is never fully implemented, the coordinator is fired, and the coach says the philosophy will not change. Matters were spinning out of control at Auburn.

"They were all upset because we lost to Vanderbilt, 14–12. I got fired after that game," Franklin said. "Never mind that it was the best Vanderbilt team in twenty-six years and we caught them in the first half of the season when they were at their best.

"It's just something that happens. You have be on board, fully on board, to make an offense work, and that isn't just the spread, that's any offense. All I know, looking back on it, is that we were 5-2 when I was there and they were 1-5 after I left, so I guess even with the mutiny we had on the staff, it must not have been all bad."

At the end of the year Tuberville resigned. He hasn't chosen to elaborate on what happened in 2008, why the spread wasn't continued, and what happened with Franklin and the rest of the staff.

Following Tuberville's departure, and the preservation of the school's grand running tradition, Auburn fell into an ironic national championship after it hired a former defensive coordinator, Gene Chizik, who then brought in Gus Malzahn as the offensive coordinator. Malzahn came from a different coaching background than Franklin but they are both spread proponents; each prefers an up-tempo, no-huddle approach. In the two previous years at Tulsa, Malzahn's offense was ranked first and second in the NCAA in total offense.

When quarterback Cam Newton transferred in after winning a national junior college championship at Blinn in Texas—Newton had been at Florida with Tim Tebow, but he transferred out after being charged with theft of a laptop computer—he fit Malzahn's frenetic spread offense better than anyone has, or maybe ever will.

The Tigers were perfect in 2010, winning the national championship against another no-huddle, fast-paced team, Oregon. Newton won the Heisman Trophy and was the first selection in the 2011 draft, signing with the Carolina Panthers.

Newton broke virtually all rookie passing records with the Panthers and his skills as a runner and an accomplished thrower may be rewriting the way coaches think of the quarterback position. Without the spread offense, chances are very good Newton would not have been a quarterback, but now there are six-foot-six, 250-pound guys who might have been considered tight ends ten years ago, who see themselves as quarterbacks.

Somebody at Auburn might have finally realized mistakes were made with Franklin, no matter the tradition. Some southerners still haven't gotten over the Civil War, and Franklin's hire represented historic change at a place where past accomplishments are always good conversation starters.

Bob Davie was in a hotel room on Thursday, November 20, 2008. He had just arrived to prepare for a game he would broadcast on Saturday when his phone rang. It was Urban Meyer, calling from Gainesville, wondering if Davie was watching the ESPN game that night that matched Georgia Tech and Miami.

"Oh, yeah," Davie said, "I got it on. I remember what it was like."

Georgia Tech was in the middle of an eventual 41–23 victory over the Hurricanes, rolling up obscene chunks of yardage with its triple-option offense installed by Coach Paul Johnson. By the time it was over, Tech would have 472 rushing yards and four rushing touchdowns. It passed the ball seven times and completed four for 46 yards.

"I'm sick to my stomach," Meyer said, "because I'm thinking back to when we were at Notre Dame and how hard it was all week for you coaches on defense to prepare for this stuff. It looks like it might be coming back."

It might, but the triple-option offense isn't likely to ever again have the appeal it once had because it's not one of those offenses that draws talent like a magnet. It's one that takes the fun out of practice and diminishes quarterbacks and receivers who aspire to play in the NFL. But it is effective and you can win with it if a coach, like Johnson, has the temerity to give it a try. It wears opponents out in preparation, just as Urban Meyer's offense made them stay up late at night at Florida.

The difference is, with the spread, players want to be a part of it; with the triple option, they want to play if they don't have the opportunity to play in the spread. From the very start, the spread has been tricky to defend and fun to play in and watch, which is why it won't be going away any time soon.

15

Full Circle (2012)

Sometimes things just work out for the best, no matter the detour and sidesteps along the way.

Dennis Erickson introduced the spread offense at Washington State in 1987 when he thought he had arrived at his destination job. Two years later he was gone, and you can't blame a guy for leaving what had been a straggler in the Pacific-10 Conference for Miami, one of the three or four top national powers of the day.

His old high school teammate Mike Price followed Erickson, getting the Cougars to Rose Bowls in 1997 and 2002, and in every season since Erickson arrived Washington State has used the spread offense to move the football. In recent times the schemes didn't look as impressive, following recruiting losses for NCAA sanctions that occurred after Price left.

But during the 2011 season the school's director of athletics, Bill Moos, the former Cougar who was schooled by a young John Elway on a backyard basketball hoop was looking for a coach. The Spread evolved from Erickson's original concept to an option component with a quarterback running to an up-tempo approach, and others that used some of this and some of that. In 2011 Paul Wulff, a center who played on Erickson's teams in Pullman, was the fourth-year coach trying to convince the fan base the program was headed in the right direction. After scholarships losses and a bad season that forced another coach out, the WSU administration was willing to give Wulff some time, but it was running short.

The Cougars started out 3-1 before a three-point loss to UCLA in Pasadena that was followed by a 44–14 thrashing at home to Stanford, a bigger, tougher, more physical team that shoved Washington State all around on its home field. Next up came the Seattle Game, an annual contest played in the stadium of the NFL's Seattle Seahawks, for the benefit of WSU fans on the west side of the Cascade mountains. It's a big game in a big setting and the team is expected to be up for it.

Instead, Oregon State crushed the Cougars 44–21, and to make matters worse, Washington State lost quarterback Jeff Tuel to a separated shoulder in the second half. The Cougars had no answers and looked like they weren't ready to play. The whole unsightly mess moved Moos to make the necessary improvements sooner rather than later.

Moos came to Washington State from the athletic director's chair at Oregon, where he gained a reputation as a smart departmental leader who completely understood the issues and demands of the coaches and was able to work with them effectively while bringing administrative goals in focus at the same time. He called a friend he knew in Eugene who had a good working relationship with agents. No one understands the Pullman culture, its fan base, and its potential more than Moos and he wanted to see if Mike Leach would be interested in coaching again.

"I've always been a fan of his and that offense," Moos said. "It sort of fits in with us, it's the thing that gets your attention and makes your coaches work late into the night. I wanted that guy for a long time.

"Could I get him?" Moos said. "Would he be interested? Could I get a foot in the door? That's what I had to find out first, before we did anything else."

Word came back that, if there were an opening, Leach would like to talk about the possibilities at Washington State but he wouldn't discuss a job at a place that still had a coach. Had the new Pacific-12 Conference commissioner not been able to forge a $3 billion broadcast deal, Moos would have been like every other Cougars' AD over the years, looking for the next rising coach at a program not too far away.

Instead, the new broadcast deal had Moos instigating a plan to enlarge forty-year-old Martin Stadium with the addition of suites, luxury boxes, club seats, and a completely remodeled and expanded press box. After the 2012 Apple Cup game, plans were in place to construct a new end zone facility to house all the football staff and its training and meeting necessities, plus add more luxury seats and a giant replay screen. Moos thought Leach, the most visible proponent of the extreme possibilities of the spread offense, would fit in nicely in the new setting.

Leach was living in Key West, Florida, doing a Sirius satellite radio talk show with former ABC sideline reporter Jack Arute, wondering when and where he might find his way back into coaching after being dismissed at Texas Tech in a nasty fight with the administration. After his offense helped Oklahoma get back on its feet in his one year there in 1999, Leach accepted the job at Texas Tech and turned that offense into a record-breaking beast that began challenging for the Big 12 Conference championship by beating all the teams against which it historically struggled. When Leach came in the offense was unhinged, every square foot of the field was exploited, and the Red Raiders were selling out the stadium and going to bowl games.

The issues he had with administrators are better detailed

elsewhere, but it's fair to say the upper reaches of campus authority appeared to have a revolving door during Leach's time there, some agreeing with, others disagreeing with the athletic director or with Leach. There were never NCAA issues, just internal politics at a school that had seen a dramatic upturn in its national profile. Sometimes when programs start winning, instead of making the existing problems disappear, it brings them to the surface.

For most administrations, engaging in conversations about employment with Mike Leach can require a bit of faith and maybe a couple of crossed fingers. From any view, he's not a mainstream guy, from his background in Cody, Wyoming, born into a Mormon family, to his fascination with the culture of eighteenth-century pirates such as Calico Jack, the one who came up with the classic Jolly Roger flag, a skull above crossed swords. Leach was impressed by the functionality of pirates and how they broke out of the caste system in England. "It didn't matter what you were," Leach said, "didn't matter your color, religion, none of that; if you were a pirate, you were part of a team with a goal. If stuff wasn't working out, you could always overthrow the captain and let somebody else take over." He liked the fundamentals, namely that pirates were on a mission to find treasure and if they did, they split it up and everybody was happy. Get the damn treasure, that was the focus.

His teams won every year at Texas Tech, though they were just 3-5 in the conference in Leach's first season in 2000. They finished 7-6 and went to a bowl game and from there on they began to pick up momentum.

In his third year at Tech Leach coached the team to a Tangerine Bowl date with Clemson that developed into a 55–15 rout that was distinguished more by the Red Raiders' defense than anything else. The Tigers couldn't stop Texas Tech. Worse, they couldn't move the ball themselves and the last quarter is remembered more for the ferocious beating taken by Clemson quarterback Charlie Whitehurst than anything else.

Leach's memory of the game? "I remember watching Whitehurst before the game on the field and then in the first half," he said. "That was a pretty talented kid; I would have liked to have had a chance to work with a guy like that."

Comparative statistics in college aren't always reliable because there are so many variables on teams from coast to coast and the talent levels go up and down by region and by conference. But it is at least noteworthy to see what Leach has managed to get out of his college quarterbacks, who don't always transition well to the professional game. An exception to that might have been Tim Couch, who Leach coached at Kentucky. Couch was the first overall player taken in the 1999 draft, but shoulder injuries eventually cost him his career.

Kliff Kingsbury is more similar to Leach quarterbacks over the years. At Tech, he played forty-three games, passed for 12,429 yards, and had ninety-five touchdowns, and forty interceptions. Whitehurst, that quarterback Leach liked when he saw him at the bowl game in Orlando, played in forty-three Clemson games, passed for 9,665 yards, and had forty-nine touchdowns and forty-six interceptions.

As the 2013 NFL off-season progressed, Whitehurst was still in the league, albeit as a well-paid backup with the San Diego Chargers, while Kingsbury wasn't able to sustain his professional career past a 2007 season in the Canadian Football League. Leach surely has a way, an insight, with his players that works awfully well in college.

In 2004 the power of Leach's offense was displayed in a win over TCU when the Horned Frogs had a 21–0 lead with eight minutes left in the second quarter on Tech's home field. It was around that point that Leach's offense began to click off touchdowns. There were ten of them after that early deficit in an eventual 70–35 win that rattled around and made noise that wouldn't go away—ten touchdowns in less than thirty-eight minutes of playing time?

It was fortunate for the Horned Frogs that their hosts got off to a slow start that day. Later in the same season, Tech beat Nebraska 70–10, scoring more points than anyone had in the history of the Cornhuskers' program.

Some schools backed away from Leach rather than sort through the issues and make a determination about how well he might fit. At one point in 2010, rumors were strong that the University of Maryland would offer Leach its job, but the Terrapins eventually chose Randy Edsall, Connecticut's coach, to rebuild hope and sell tickets again in a competitive sports market. Instead, Maryland went 2-10 in Edsall's first season, players were transferring, and attendance was down.

Here was Moos, who knows the school and the market as well as anyone—he drives to Spokane and back once a week for a radio show—flying to Key West to see if a football coach living there would be a good fit. "The first thing I learned," Moos said, "is that there are no direct flights from Pullman to Key West."

It took all day, but the next morning Moos called and Leach went to see him, in a T-shirt, shorts, and flip-flops, on his bicycle. "It would have been a good picture," Moos said. "I'm wearing a Hart Schaffner Marx suit—probably a little overdressed—and some expensive shoes and all, and here's Mike dressing the way you dress in Key West."

Moos talked about the school president being on board with everything he was going to discuss, he brought artist's renderings of the stadium addition with the suites and club seats and the plans for the end zone facilities with all the coaches' offices, weight and meeting rooms, and all the rest.

"People out there in public, the fans? They might not have ever heard of Bill Moos," Leach said, "but coaches know about him, I can promise you that. He's one of those guys you would hear about in coaching circles, it would be in a conversation about ADs who get it, something like that, and Bill's name would always come up. He does it right, he's honest with you, and really, that's all you can ask."

Leach has a somewhat similar personal profile. A law degree from Pepperdine University gave him a different way of looking at things, sizing up issues, and making decisions. In his book *Swing Your Sword*, Leach indicated how he applied what he learned in law school to his football career: "During my first orientation at Pepperdine, one of the professors said that as a law student, you won't be getting a degree in case memorization or rule memorization. Instead, you learn how to take a variety of facts and a certain amount of precedent and apply them to the problem at hand. You are actually getting a degree in problem solving. Well, football certainly supplies a lot of problems to solve."

Leach solved a lot of them at Texas Tech and Moos was feeling like they were a match minutes after they met. They were finishing each other's sentences and agreeing on just about everything.

"It had probably been ninety minutes or so," Moos said, "and it was going great. I have this thing about discipline on the team, about being up front, transparent, whatever you want to call it, and I asked what he thought about a three-strike rule for kids getting in trouble.

"Even with pot," Moos said. "I know it's not the biggest issue, but even with that, I think you have to draw a line. I asked what he thought about it and for just a moment I had an *uh-oh* sensation, like I asked the wrong thing."

"That brought us close," Leach said later of the moment. "Bill mentioned three strikes and I said, 'I don't know about that; what do you think of a one-strike policy?'" Leach then explained he had three things that would get players off the roster immediately — hitting a woman, using drugs, and not being a serious student in the classroom.

"You get pot smokers, that will split the locker room in a minute," Leach said. "I don't want that shit going on and I'll let them know about it, probably in the first minute of the first meeting we have."

Outwardly, Moos smiled and said they could make that plan work. Inside, he was ecstatic. He figured a few players might not make it under the Leach guidelines, but he hoped he was wrong.

He wasn't wrong.

"His plan works," Moos said prior to Leach's first Washington State fall camp in 2012. "I'm not sure we have any linebackers left on our roster, but the plan works."

By the first week of March, four months after Leach accepted the job and was named the new Cougars' coach, the only scholarship linebackers in the program, Sekope Kaufusi and C. J. Mizell, were each dismissed from the team. Kaufusi was arrested by Pullman police when he was found in possession of marijuana and drug paraphernalia after they served a search warrant on his apartment. Mizell was dismissed earlier, after being arrested on suspicion of misdemeanor assault and trespassing at a fraternity party.

Washington State went into its first season under Mike Leach without a scholarship linebacker on the roster. No linebackers in fall camp that season had ever started a college football game. The Pirate, as he is known for his fascination with all things pirate, had his system of corrections in place.

What was it like when Leach spoke to the team for the first time? What was the message, what was his approach?

"Kind of odd," said Tuel, the returning quarterback. "Impressive, no doubt, but I didn't expect he would start by telling us in the first minute he spoke about the three things that will get you kicked off the team. He made it real clear, real fast that this was going to be a serious approach.

"Everybody got the message," Tuel said. "Well, almost everybody, I guess, but everyone here now gets it."

It's the same with the spread, or what passes for the spread these days, since the original design from Neumeier and Elway has been refined, remade, restructured, reinvented so many times you can barely find the base concept in today's offensive systems. That's not a criticism, it's really a laudatory view of what's happened since 1970. Back then, the idea was to take advantage of the defensive deficiencies of the day. Defenses were big and built to stop the run. Linebackers had upper bodies to bring the blows at the point of attack but they didn't have skill sets that matched up with pass-coverage techniques, so the spread went directly at those positions and forced players to do something foreign to what they knew.

The best linebackers of the day, people like Mike Singletary, could be picked apart and abused by the spread, but over time, as more teams began spreading out in high school and college, coaches looked for a different breed of linebacker. In order to cover the different array of receivers, from the tall kids who used to play basketball until they saw the spread to the kids who were thought to be too small until they realized they could find a role in a five-receiver pass pattern, defensive players started matching the body types of the offense.

A new kind of defensive position, a robber, bandit, joker—there are dozens of different terms for the position—was developed. The position was part linebacker, part safety, part pass rusher, and the player was usually positioned on the outside, standing up like a linebacker. Sometimes the player would line up in more of a safety position, then walk up to the line as the snap count progressed or move into a coverage or rush situation just before the snap. Defenses are lighter now, quicker, and they are more well versed at covering pass patterns, which is why there's been an offensive wrinkle, sending some teams like Stanford to a pro-style power offense approach that knuckles down and muscles up on lighter defenses, but the spread isn't going away any time soon.

Opponents reacted to the lighter defenses by not huddling and playing faster, leaving less time between snaps to make it harder for the defense to change personnel. Then, when they did change personnel, the offense, because they ran plays fast, had enough time to change their play and take advantage of the players who just entered.

Leach, in his book, recounted how he and Mumme would sit in a Mount Pleasant, Iowa, café and dream up plays. "There's no way you can say we copied this or we copied that," Mumme said, "because we took from everything that was out there but there was hardly a one of them that we just left; we'd take a BYU pass play and tweak the route, we'd use principles from here, principles from there and put 'em together to make something new."

Leach remembered "a lot of it, early on," being from the BYU playbook because they were both familiar with it, but his memory mirrors Mumme's in that they always did something to call it their own and when they were done it was the air raid. "I've never been too much on terms and names for things and all that," Leach said. "I want production and you can call it anything you want as far as I'm concerned."

The longer he was a head coach, the more refined he became. At Texas Tech he made up a playbook for the assistant coaches, a move he second-guessed later on. "For them, I thought it would help them refer back to the few plays we had were there any questions, but you really don't need it," he said.

We don't believe in a lot of plays because the one thing you can control, in my opinion, is the proficiency with which you execute your plays.

If we have four running plays and we rep them constantly, we can get pretty good at those plays. The defense doesn't know what the play is going to be because you spend a lot of time mixing up your formations. It's a lot easier and it works a lot better to have just a few plays and a wide variety of formations, you can confuse the defense some, but when it gets to running the play, you know what you're doing.

Leach seems the ideal capstone to decades of spread football offenses at Washington State. The offense Erickson used when he was there would look similar in some ways to what Leach puts on the field, but times have changed. Teams play faster now; defenses aren't burly and slow like the ones Erickson's Cougars picked apart.

"The goals haven't changed at all with what we want to do," Leach said.

You have to make the defense cover the field horizontally and you have make them cover it vertically. I've never worried too much about balance when they talk about "You need to run this may times," or "You can't be passing it *that* much," you know how they talk when they don't really get it.

To me, balance means getting the ball to all your guys, so if you have four or five receivers and a running back who all need it, spread it around some. It doesn't mean the one running back needs to get it as many times as all the receivers, that's not balance.

Moos and Leach found in each other just what they had been looking for on their own. "I always loved that offense of his every time I saw it," Moos said. "It was like what we do here, only newer. I always thought it would be great to have a coach like him, but until we got these new [broadcasting] deals, there wasn't going to be much opportunity. The way it is now? Let's go."

Leach spent ten years at Texas Tech and, about three years into it, had lifted the program to the highest level. At Washington State, the stadium is being enlarged and six 3-D cameras have been installed in permanent locations to record every move of what happens on the Martin Field turf. Memories of Rose Bowls, despite the recent decline, are not that distant.

"This is a great place," Leach said in his office before the start of 2012 fall camp, "a great place for us, that's for sure. Did you know this land, this area, the Palouse, was formed in the Ice Age and the silt that came from it is why it's so good for growing wheat and lentils?

"Not many places in the country do more in-depth research on grizzly bears than right here," Leach added. "Is that great, or what?"

Before his first season, he was as enthused as he's ever been about coaching, even while he took note of the latest wrinkles to the spread approach—up-tempo pace and no huddle. "That's all good, we always tend to play with a rhythm, you want that, always," he said. "This concept about 'using the clock' is one I never understood too much. What's the clock? Why are you paying so much attention to the clock? Do you look at the scoreboard part up there? That's where you win the game, not on the clock."

His philosophy is simple. Leach has ways to get the ball to virtually every spot on the field, horizontally and vertically. Technically, not every spot is always open because a pass has to be out in about three seconds, so a deep pass might go about 40 yards in the air, which is plenty.

"Here's what I think about the clock," Leach said. "If I get the ball at my 20 and I go through your defense in three or four plays to get a touchdown, I'm not thinking about the clock, I'm thinking, 'I wonder if we got lucky there—that does happen, both ways—or I wonder if these guys just can't defend our offense.'

"Next time we get the ball, we're going to try to score in three or four more plays," he said, "and if we do that, I'm going to start thinking you can't stop us, so I'm not going to think about slowing it down; let's go score some more points.

"The clock doesn't figure in too much, unless it's an end-of-game situation," he said. "If I look out from the sidelines and see my quarterback out there, standing up, looking around, tickling the center's ass, that doesn't do much for me."

But these things are done with a confidence that has been built on a framework of success in the SEC, the Big 12, and now the Pac-12, where Leach will confront some of the most explosive and high-scoring spread offenses of the day, starting with Oregon's under former Coach Chip Kelly, who started coaching in the 1990s, became the offensive coordinator at New Hampshire, and was among the first to get his teams playing in a sprint. In 2013 he will take his insights to the NFL's Philadelphia Eagles, who hired him in the offseason. Oregon became a national power behind Kelly's guidance and his efforts are continually recognized with coaching awards and honors, just as the Ducks have been playing for national championships and making their marks in big-time games.

Even Kelly, age forty-nine prior to the start of the 2013 season, has seen a newer wave of spread coaches influencing the game. Just the other day he was the new guy on the block; now they're coming from the high school ranks, like

Art Briles, the Leach disciple at Baylor, Gus Malzahn, the offensive coordinator for Cam Newton and the spread champions at Auburn (he's now the head coach at Auburn), and Chad Morris, the former Lake Travis, Texas, high school coach who was the highest-paid offensive coordinator in the country, for Clemson, in the 2012 season.

The spread guarantees you nothing, it isn't a panacea for complacency, and it won't make bad football players good overnight. In the right hands it can still make a career-changing difference, but Hal Mumme, who brought Leach into college football, has been one of the second-wave spread coaches who's struggled at times. After the scandals ran them all out of Kentucky, Mumme was hired to coach at Southeastern Louisiana, which was restarting its program at the Division I-AA level. Two years later New Mexico called, but in Mumme's first year there the team went winless, trying to convert from an option offense as Erickson had once done at Wyoming. In four years Mumme couldn't win more than four games in a single season and he was gone soon after a lawsuit—eventually settled out of court—brought by four Muslim players accused him of creating a hostile work environment because of their religion. Mumme took a job at Division III McMurry State and was 28-13 before he stepped down following the 2012 season to join June Jones at SMU.

From Urban Meyer (Ohio State) to Dan Mullen (Mississippi State), his former sidekick, most of the coaches who jumped in with the spread in the 1990s have been successful, but Erickson's coaching career detoured with a bad season at Arizona State in 2011 that ended with his termination. At one point in the season ASU beat Southern California by three touchdowns and looked to be a top-ten team, but the Sun Devils went into a second-half tailspin when they seemed incapable of beating anybody. "I did a bad job, we all did," Erickson said before taking the offensive coordinator position at Utah. "It leaves a bad taste in your mouth."

Since he started at Wyoming in 1986, Erickson coached 216 games at the Division I level, won 143, or 66 percent, of them, with two national championships, and had the distinction of being the first coach to win a title with a spread offense. He saw something in the offense others didn't see, something he knew could work based on his understanding of football. All things equal, if you have a better idea than the other guy, you probably have an edge.

"We're going to try to do everything here," Leach said. "Win as much as we can at the highest level we can attain. What Mike Price did here [two Rose Bowls] will stand the test of time.

"There is a tradition," he said. "I've watched Dennis's teams, gained inspiration from him, attended his practices, drawn on what he's done, and my suspicion is that what we do is congruent with what he had in mind all along.

"Within coaching circles, everyone has an idea that they think can work for him, you know? Erickson has always been a guy that other coaches knew and respected, he had a way of looking at things that other coaches, I don't know, they didn't know where to look, I guess."

Leach is in the heart of the place that brought the spread to life in college football, and now that the forty-year-old stadium is undergoing a transformation, there's a sense that the stage is set for something more. Erickson showed how to win there, Price got them to the Rose Bowl, and Leach?

"We want to do it all," he said.

If you watch his team, or most any good spread team, you probably will see the ball in the air more than at some other games, for a good reason. "I guess it's my personality type," Leach said of his belief in the forward pass.

Some guys think if you run the ball and get no yards, that's somehow more beneficial than throwing an incomplete pass. I understand that you can have a running play that can go as long as a pass, but if I need 10 yards, my personality tells me I have a better chance of getting that in one play with the pass than I do of getting it with a running play.

If you can complete more than 50 percent of your passes, and we typically get close to 70 percent, you're just going to have more success that way, on balance, than being a heavy run team.

Remember, offense is an exercise in creating space, while defense is an exercise in restricting space. If you can create more space before the snap with formation or motion or both, then you need to do that.

Leach didn't know that informal tribe of Northwest coaches led by Jack Swarthout who were always looking for a better way, willing to take a chance on something new if it made sense to them, but he was one of them just the same. So were Tony Franklin, Gus Malzahn, Chad Morris, Urban Meyer, and all the others. In the congested circle of coaching concepts, overlapping and replicating each other, they knew there was a better way.

They just needed to find a way to spread out and find unprotected space in the defense. That's where the ball will go.

Notes

1. HOME OF THE CHOKERS (LATE 1940s)

1   **Swarthout was something of:** Dee Hawkes, interview by author, 2009; Bob Beers, interview by author, 2010.

4   **They weren't just looking:** John Sayle Watterson, *College Football: History, Spectacle, Controversy* (Baltimore: Johns Hopkins University Press, 2000): 206.

5   **The area had been inhabited:** Jacilee Wray, *Native Peoples of the Olympic Peninsula: Who We Are* (Norman: University of Oklahoma Press, 2002).

7   **He knew it all starts:** Beers interview, 2010.

9   **"We're going to do it over":** Beers interview, 2010.

10   **They were banned on a:** John C. Hughes, *On the Harbor: From Black Friday to Nirvana* (Aberdeen WA: Daily World, 2001).

12   **Swarthout was nothing like that:** James W. Johnson, *The Wow Boys: A Coach, a Team, and a Turning Point in College Football* (Lincoln: University of Nebraska Press, 2006.

2. TEAM STARTS WITH *T* (LATE 1940s, EARLY 1950s)

17   **Swarthout said coaching Elway:** Beers interview, 2010.

20   **"I'm not sure what":** Vince Dooley, interview by author, 2009.

21   **Instead, Shaughnessy had the ear:** Johnson, *Wow Boys.*

22   **Some hire for Stanford:** Johnson, *Wow Boys.*

23   **"Swarthout was the leader":** Beers interview, 2010.

23   **His father, a plumber:** Joe Tiller, interview by author, 2008.

24   **"He was a helluva quarterback":** Bob Klock, interview by author, 2007.

3. HIGH SCHOOL FOOTBALL (EARLY 1950s)

25 **It was an area seen as:** Edward C. Whitman, "The Forgotten Theater: U.S. Submarine Operations in the Aleutians in World War II," *Undersea Warfare*, spring 2003, http://www.navy.mil/navydata/cno/n87/usw/issue_18/forgotten.htm.

28 **Before Erickson arrived:** "1st Battalion 30th Field Artillery," Hard Chargers of the 30th Field Artillery Regiment Association, www.heritage.hardchargers.com.

29 **He was the grand marshal:** Christy Erickson, interview by author, 2004.

30 **"I don't think I ever wanted":** Beers interview, 2010.

31 **Had he not been injured:** Rod Commons (Washington State sports information director), interview by author, 2003, 2004, 2005.

31 **When he left Washington State:** Mark Dukes and Gus Schrader, *Greatest Moments in Iowa Hawkeyes Football History* (Chicago: Triumph, 1998).

31 **After his injuries forced:** Klock interview, 2007.

33 **"Jack was always looking":** Gary Gagnon, interview by author, winter, spring 2009.

4. BIG-TIME COLLEGE FOOTBALL (MID TO LATE 1950s)

37 **Worse, the great years:** Roscoe C. Torrance, with Robert F. Karolevitz, *Torchy!: The Biography and Reminiscences of Roscoe C. Torrance* (Mission Hill SD: Dakota Homestead Publishers, 1988).

37 **McElhenny later famously said:** Richard Linde, "Scandal in the Fifties," 2002, www.4malaumte.com.

38 **"We had one play where":** Gagnon interview, winter, spring 2009.

40 **"He always said":** Beers interview, 2010.

40 **"First, he loved to laugh":** Klock interview, 2007.

44 **"We just didn't talk":** Dennis Erickson, interview by author, winter 2004.

45 **Price came back to start:** Mike Price, interview by author, 2009.

47 **"I wanted to see him":** Jim Sweeney, interview by author, 1995, 1997, 2004, 2006, 2007.

5. BEAR BRYANT AND THE COMING OF THE WISHBONE (LATE 1960s)

49 **"He was as tough":** Mal Moore, interview by author, spring 2008.

49 **There's a little-known story:** Sweeney interview, 1995, 1997, 2004, 2006, 2007.

52 **Sweeney said Erickson "was a coach":** Sweeney interview, summer 2002.

55 **"It's funny, thinking back":** Sam Jankovich, interview by author, fall 2002.

56 **"Whattaya doin' that for?":** Sweeney interview, spring 2002.

59 **"That next year":** Beers interview, spring 2007.

6. BASKETBALL ON GRASS (1970s)

63 **But Neumeier wasn't a run-and-shoot guy:** Darrell "Mouse" Davis, interview by author, 2008.

64 **"I don't think I ever met":** Davis interview, fall 2006.

64 **Neumeier thought slotbacks attracted:** Jack Neumeier, interview by author, 1995–96.

68 **"He pulled me aside":** Dana Potter, interview by author, fall 2009.

70 **"The quarterback takes one step":** Neumeier interview, 1996.

70 **"It was a totally new concept":** Quoted by David Wharton, *70 Angeles Times*, January 1, 1998.

70 **"They started up the first":** Potter interview, fall 2009.

72 **"We went from designed":** Neumeier interview, 1996.

73 **"The spread offense":** John Elway, interview by author, winter 2007.

7. PICKING ON MIKE SINGLETARY (MID TO LATE 1970s)

75 **For Sweeney, the veer was:** Sweeney interview, 1995, 1997, 2004, 2006, 2007.

77 **"In 1973, I was":** Bill Moos, interview by author, 2012.

78 **At Fresno State, one of:** Sweeney interview, 1995, 1997, 2004, 2006, 2007.

79 **"Dad loved to talk":** Elway interview, winter 2007.

82 **Green was appalled:** Bruce Feldman, *'Cane Mutiny: How the Miami Hurricanes Overturned the Football Establishment* (New York: New American Library, 2003).

83 **Green began scouring the country:** Feldman, *'Cane Mutiny.*

85 **Walsh's was a short-passing game:** Bill Walsh, *The Score Takes Care of Itself: My Philosophy of Leadership* (New York: Portfolio, 2009).

87 **"I distinctly remember"**: Beers interview, spring 2007.

88 **"If it was a noon kickoff"**: Steve Clarkson, interview by author, summer 2008.

90 **"What I remember was"**: Mike Singletary, interview by author, spring 2009.

92 **"San Jose State built"**: Clarkson interview, summer 2008.

92 **"They throw the quick stuff"**: San Jose State University archives, newspaper clipping quoting Grant Teaff.

92 **"This," he said**: San Jose State University archives, newspaper clipping quoting Jack Elway.

8. BREAKING OUT (EARLY 1980S)

96 **"When he left to go"**: Clarkson interview, summer 2008

99 **It became the new sacred**: Howard Schnellenberger, interview by author, 2006.

100 **"I can't tell you why"**: Schnellenberger interview, 2006.

104 **"Everybody was talking"**: Keith Gilbertson, interview by author, summer 2008.

105 **"It was so new"**: Scott Linehan, interview by author, winter 2010.

107 **"He pulled me out"**: Tim Lappano, interview by author, summer 2007.

108 **"I'll never forget"**: Dan Cozzetto, interview by author, fall 2006.

9. TURNING POINT (LATE 1980S)

111 **"I wasn't going"**: Jankovich interview, summer 2006.

114 **They were comfortable in chaos**: Brian Blades, interview by author, 1995, 1996.

115 **"I was astonished"**: Jankovich interview, summer 2006.

117 **"Dennis brought an offense"**: Gilbertson interview, summer 2008.

118 **"He was young looking"**: Eric Yarber, interview by author, summer 2008.

119 **"The final score"**: Gilbertson interview, 2006.

121 **But that day years later**: Dee Andros, interview by author, 1999.

10. SETTLING IN AND GETTING OUT (LATE 1980S, EARLY 1990S)

123 **As soon as he arrived**: Gil Brandt, interview by author, March 2008.

123 **"I said hi":** Jankovich interview, summer 2006.

124 **"I never demanded anything":** Jankovich interview, summer 2006.

125 **"He brought in Butch":** Jankovich interview, summer 2006.

129 **"It was all about":** Timm Rosenbach, interview by author, winter 2010.

129 **"I was amazed":** Dennis Erickson interview, summer 2010.

131 **"He said my teammates":** Rosenbach interview, winter 2010.

132 **"People were just calling it":** Noel Mazzone, interview by author, summer 2011.

133 He was one of those: Jimmy Johnson, *Turning the Thing Around: My Life in Football* (New York: Hyperion, 1993).

137 **"On occasion," the player said:** Michael Weinreb, "The Night College Football Went to Hell," ESPN: *The Magazine*, December 1, 2009.

137 **"We didn't sit down":**Jim Martz, *Tales from the Miami Hurricanes Sideline* (Champaign IL: Sports Publishing, 2004), 141

138 **"That might have happened":** Brandt interview, fall 2009.

11. CHANGES, EVEN IN THE SOUTH (1990s)

140 **"I don't like that term":** Mike Smith, interview by author, fall 2011.

141 **"In one, they had":** Kevin Steele, interview by author, summer 2009.

148 **"I questioned it":** Tommy Tuberville, interview by author, summer 2007.

148 **"Those players educated me":** Dennis Erickson interview, summer 2011.

150 **"There were so many":** Edwin Pope, interview by author, spring 2010.

155 The week before the game: *Miami Herald*.

156 The atmosphere Erickson entered: Personal observations at Super Bowl XXIII; Cortez Kennedy, interview by author, 2009.

12. HERE IT COMES, HIDDEN IN PLAIN SIGHT (MID-1990s)

159 **"I don't think anyone":** Dan LeBatard, interview by author, fall 2010.

160 Tuberville wondered if Miami: Tuberville interview, 2003.

161 Twice Erickson had declined: Dennis Erickson interview, 1989.

162   "Dennis, you can win": Jankovich interview, 2004.

162   Mumme was at home: Hal Mumme, interview by author, 2006.

165   "It wasn't us": Dennis Erickson interview, summer 2010.

167   "[Erickson] told me": Kennedy interview, fall 2011.

168   "I never liked taunting": Dennis Erickson interview, summer 2010.

169   "All I remember is": Dennis Erickson interview, spring 2009.

169   "It was the only job": Bobby Bowden, interview by author, fall 2009.

170   "It was a big secret": Tommy Bowden, interview by author, fall 2006.

171   "I remember in 1987": Bob Davie, interview by author, fall 2009.

172   "[Defensive coordinator] Ken Donahue": Steele interview, summer 2009.

174   "Do I remember?": Gary Pinkel, interview by author, fall 2012.

175   "We had a look": Steele interview, summer 2009.

175   "I was trying": Don James, interview by author, fall 2009.

176   "That was the first time": Steele interview, summer 2009.

13. HERE, THERE, EVERYWHERE (LATE 1990S, EARLY 2000S)

179   "We were allowed to": Mumme interview, summer 2010.

181   "I had a couple kids": Tony Franklin, interview by author, fall 2011.

182   Iowa Wesleyan lost the game: Iowa Wesleyan Sports Information Department, interview by author; *Iowa City Press-Citizen*, September 13, 2010.

185   "Back then we would fling it": Steve Spurrier, interview by author, fall 2011.

185   Spurrier's decision to hire: Spurrier interview, 2010.

187   "It wasn't instant": Bob Stoops, interview by author, spring 2010.

188   "We just had a heck": Stoops interview, spring 2010.

188   "Luther was a good guy": Dennis Erickson interview, spring 2009.

189   Federal officials referred to it: "Why the University of Miami Should Drop Football," *Sports Illustrated*, June 12, 1995, 22.

189   "Of all the stuff": Dennis Erickson interview, spring 2009.

191   "From the first day": Dennis Erickson interview, winter 2003.

193   "He was the guy who": Davie interview, fall 2009.

193   "We kicked around ideas": Dan Mullen, interview by author, winter 2010.

193   They borrowed some of the Syracuse playbook: Davie interview, 2009.

195   Meyer said he first remembered: Urban Meyer, interview by author, 2008.

196   "Our defense created": Bill Snyder, interview by author, fall 2009.

197   "It wasn't a distraction": Davie interview, fall 2009.

14. SPIRIT OF A NEW MILLENNIUM (2000s)

200   Andros saw the game change: Andros interview, 1999.

201   Johnson had everything coaches look for: Yarber interview, 2006, 2007.

201   "I was watching him": Yarber interview, fall 2008.

202   "I wanted to see": Dennis Erickson interview, spring 2009.

202   "We all liked Riley": Jonathan Smith, interview by author, summer 2006.

204   "Probably coaches say this": Dennis Erickson interview, spring 2009.

204   "They were going wild": Cozzetto interview, summer 2006.

205   "He was in complete control": Andros interview, summer 2000.

206   "I'll tell you what": Davie interview, fall 2009.

213   "Everybody was nice": Franklin interview, fall 2011.

15. FULL CIRCLE (2012)

220   The whole unsightly mess: Moos interview, July 2012.

220   "I've always been": Moos interview, summer 2012.

222   "It didn't matter": Mike Leach, interview by author, summer 2012.

224   "The first thing I learned": Moos interview, summer 2012.

225   "People out there": Leach interview, summer 2012.

225   "It had probably": Moos interview, summer 2012.

225   "That brought us close": Leach interview, summer 2012.

226   "His plan works": Moos interview, summer 2012.

226   "Kind of odd": Jeff Tuel, interview by author, summer 2009.

228   **Leach remembered "a lot of it":** Leach interview, summer 2012.

230   **"I always loved":** Moos interview, summer 2012.

230   **"This is a great place":** Leach interview, summer 2012.

233   **"I did a bad job":** Dennis Erickson interview, winter 2012.

233   **"We're going to try":** Leach interview, summer 2012.